ISBN 978-1-330-58786-7
PIBN 10041743

1 MONTH OF
FREE
READING

at

www.ForgottenBooks.com

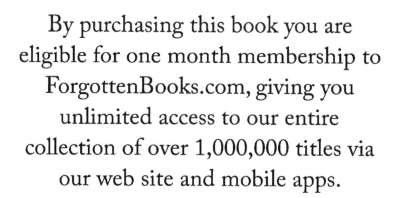

By purchasing this book you are eligible for one month membership to ForgottenBooks.com, giving you unlimited access to our entire collection of over 1,000,000 titles via our web site and mobile apps.

To claim your free month visit:
www.forgottenbooks.com/free41743

English
Français
Deutsche
Italiano
Español
Português

www.forgottenbooks.com

Mythology Photography **Fiction**
Fishing Christianity **Art** Cooking
Essays Buddhism Freemasonry
Medicine **Biology** Music **Ancient**
Egypt Evolution Carpentry Physics
Dance Geology **Mathematics** Fitness
Shakespeare **Folklore** Yoga Marketing
Confidence Immortality Biographies
Poetry **Psychology** Witchcraft
Electronics Chemistry History **Law**
Accounting **Philosophy** Anthropology
Alchemy Drama Quantum Mechanics
Atheism Sexual Health **Ancient History**
Entrepreneurship Languages Sport
Paleontology Needlework Islam
Metaphysics Investment Archaeology
Parenting Statistics Criminology
Motivational

THE

Religious State.

BY

MICHAEL MÜLLER,

Priest of the Congregation of the Most Holy Redeemer.

BALTIMORE:

KREUZER BROTHERS,

CATHOLIC PUBLISHERS, BOOKSELLERS, &C.

1872.

Entered, according to Act of Congress, in the year 1871, by
KREUZER BROTHERS,
in the Office of the Librarian of Congress, at Washington.

CONTENTS.

CHAPTER I.

A CERTAIN traveler came one evening to the entrance of a vast forest. The sun was just setting, but yet he could neither tarry nor retrace his steps. He was obliged to pass through the forest amid the darkness of the night. As he was about to enter these gloomy woods, he beheld an old man of venerable aspect, of whom he inquired the way. The good old man was a shepherd. "Alas," said the old man, "it is not easy to show you the way. The forest is traversed by a thousand paths that cross one another and turn in every direction, and yet though they sometimes resemble one another, they all, with one single exception, lead to a fathomless abyss." "What abyss do you mean?" asked the traveler. "I mean," answered the old man, "the abyss that surrounds the entire forest. But this is not yet all," continued he, "the forest is not safe; it is filled with robbers and wild beasts; there is particularly an enormous serpent that infests this

forest and causes the most frightful ravages. There
is scarcely a day passes but we find the mangled
remains of some unhappy traveler of whom he has
made his prey. And yet you must absolutely pass
through this forest, in order to arrive at the country
to which you are going. Touched with compassion
I have stationed myself at the entrance of this
dangerous passage, in order to guide and protect all
who enter this forest. At certain distances along
the route I have stationed my sons who are animated
with the same sentiments as myself and fulfillthe
the same offices of charity. I hereby offer you my
services and theirs and if you desire it, I will accompany you."

The air of candor of the old man and the tone of
honesty in which he spoke, inspired the traveler
with confidence ; he accepted the proposal. In one
hand the old man took his lamp and with the other
he seized the arm of the traveller, and they instantly set out on ther journey. After having travelled
for some time, the traveller began to feel that his
strength was giving way. "Lean on my shoulder,"
said his faithful guide. The traveler did so, and
thus supported, continued his journey.

Soon the light of the lamp began to grow dim,
and cast only a faint, unsteady glimmer. "Our
lamp is going out," cried the traveler in dismay;
"what shall become of us ?" "O do not fear," an-

swered the old man in a calm tone; "we shall soon arrive at the house of one of my sons and he will fill our lamp with oil." The old man spoke the truth. In a short time a torch appeared gleaming through the darkness and the traveller beheld a small but neat cottage standing on the road-side. At the well known voice of the old man the door opened; the weary traveller was invited to take a seat; a frugal but substantial meal was placed before him, and he soon regained his wonted strength. After a rest of three quarters of an hour the traveller continued his journey, accompanied now by the son of the venerable old man.

From time to time the traveller came to other cottages on his route, where he was kindly treated and where he found new guides. He thus continued his journey during the entire night.

As the first rays of the dawn illumined the horizon, the traveller arrived safely at the extremity of the dangerous forest. It was now that he fully understood for the first time the great kindness of the old man and his sons. He beheld at his feet a frightful abyss from which arose the hoarse roar of a distant torrent.

"Behold," said his guide, "the abyss of which my father spoke to you. No one knows its depth; it is always covered with a thick fog which the eye cannot penetrate." As he said these words he heaved a deep sigh and wiped off the tears that trickled down his checks.

"You seem to have some secret sorrow," said the traveller. "Alas! why should I not grieve," answered the guide. "How can I look on this abyss without thinking of the many unhappy souls that are lost there every day. It is all useless for my father and myself to speak to them and to offer them our services. Very few heed us. The greater part, after having walked for a few hours in our company, accuse us of wishing to terrify them by vain fears; they despise our warnings; they abandon us, and very soon they go astray and perish miserably; they are either devoured by the enormous serpent or assassinated by robbers, or engulfed in this frightful abyss. For, as you see, there is only this narrow bridge, over which you can cross this abyss; and we alone know the path that leads to it. Go on now courageously," said he, turning to the traveller and embracing him with tenderness; "as soon as you have crossed the bridge, you will find that it is broad day-light and that you are at home."

The traveller, filled with gratitude, thanked his charitable guide, promised that he would never forget him, crossed the bridge at a rapid pace, and was soon safe and happy in the midst of his beloved family.

Dear reader, this traveller is yourself. The dark

gloomy forest is this world, so full of trials and dangers. The cruel serpent is the devil, the enemy of souls. The robbers and assassins are your passions and temptations. The country beyond is heaven, your true home. The bridge over which you must pass to reach heaven, is the grace of a happy death. The good charitable shepherd is our Lord Jesus Christ. His children and assistants are the priests, your spiritual directors. The lamp is God's inspiration; it is the knowledge of your vocation. If this lamp should at times seem extinguished, if the oil appear to go out, you must replenish it by praying and by consulting your spiritual director. The various paths that traverse the forest are the various ''ways that seem to man to be good, but which lead to destruction.'' Prov.

The only path that leads safely and infallibly through this dangerous forest is the faithful compliance with the holy will of God; it is the faithful correspondence with the grace of your vocation.

If it is your vocation to live in the world, you must indeed not think of entering the religious state. But if it is your vocation to enter the religious life, you will run the greatest risk of losing your soul by remaining amid the dangers and temptations of the world. It is true that all are not called to the religious life; but it is also true that many are called, who do not answer the call of God. I have thought, therefore, dear reader, of writing this little book, in order to show to all who may be called to the religious life, the great value and happiness of such a vocation, the necessity of corresponding therewith, and the great danger of neglecting and abusing this signal grace.

CHAPTER II.

ST. Isidor says, that the word 'religion' is derived from the Latin expression *relegenda lege* (to read often the law of God); so that the name of 'religious' may be applied to him who often reads, reflects and meditates upon what appertains to the divine worship.

According to St. Augustine, the word 'religion' is derived from the latin word *re-eligendo* (to re-elect), because, after having lost our Lord by sin, we ought to re-elect or choose Him again as our true and only Lord and Sovereign Master. But, according to the same Saint, the word 'religion', is more properly and truly derived from *religando* (to re-unite), because it re-unites man with God, with Whom he was primitively united, but from Whom he voluntarily separated by sin. Hence, according to St. Thomas, religion' is a virtue which teaches us to live in union with God, by the practice of interior acts of adoration, of invocation,.

of reverence, &c., as well as by exterior acts, such as vows, sacrifices, genuflexions, hymns, &c. For this reason religion is, after the three theological virtues, the noblest, and the principal source of all other moral virtues, as it teaches us to worship and serve God in a worthy manner, to practise all other virtues for the sake of God, and to refer everything to Him as to the true and only cause of all good. The faithful practice of this virtue leads to sanctity, which according to St. Thomas, is the flower of religion, since sanctity makes us offer to God our soul quite pure and free from every stain of sin, and preserve for Him alone, all its strength, powers and affections. All other moral virtues are as it were, subservient to this virtue, some in as much as they purify the will, others in as much as they enlighten the mind, and others again in as much as they restrain and mortify the senses.

The fruits or chief effects of sanctity are prayer and devotion; prayer which leads the soul to familiar intercourse with God, and devotion which renders it prompt and cheerful in the performance of everything pertaining to His service. Of so great a value before God is this fervor of the will, that destitute of it, we are less agreeable to the Almighty in all the services which we render Him; but animated with it, we become most pleasing and dear in His sight.

Religion as such is the form, and the soul, as it were, of the religious state; and therefore those who embrace this state, are called *Religious*, professing, as they do, to strive after perfection and sanctity. Jesus Christ Himself is the Author of this life of perfection. His life and doctrine gave birth to the religious life. He taught the counsels and the practice of making vows. His life was the model for all those who wished to become perfect. "If thou wilt be perfect," said He to the young man in the Gospel, "go, sell what thou hast and give to the poor, and come follow Me."

Many grave authors are of opinion, that Jesus Christ Himself made the three religious vows. They grant, it is true, that Jesus Christ did not make vows for the same reason. for which we generally take them, that is, to confirm and fix our will in good (there being no inconstancy of will in Him), but that He took vows for several other reasons.

First—In order to offer to His Father the most noble act of religion, which consists in the vow of dedicating and consecrating to God, not only all that we have and do, but also our will in such a manner as neither to possess nor will anything except what He wills; thus offering to the Almighty the tree together with its fruits.

Second—Jesus Christ took vows, in order that, as master and teacher of perfection, He might be an example and model for imitation to His Apostles and to us. "Every one of you that doth not renounce all that he possesseth, cannot be My disciple." Luke XIV, 33. And in the Gospel of St. Mark chapt. X, 28, and St. Luke chapt. XVIII, 28, the Apostles openly assert that they followed the example of poverty which our Lord had given them. "Behold, we have left all things, and have followed Thee."

Third—Because it is only by vow that a perfect renunciation of the goods of this world can be made. It is by vow that we voluntarily renounce not only the goods which we actually possess, but also those which we might acquire in time to come.

Fourth—The three vows of religion are the three most excellent holocausts. But Christ offered Himself and all He had, as a most perfect holocaust, to God His Father. The opinion then is most probable, and, as such, it is embraced by Francis Suarez, Salmeron and others that Christ, in the first moment of His life, by vows offered and dedicated Himself, whole and entire, without reserve to His Heavenly Father, together with all that He possessed.

The example of Jesus Christ was followed by the Apostles, as we may gather from the words of St. Peter, who spoke in the name of all the rest when he said: "Behold we have forsaken all things and have followed Thee." *By all things*, their wives are also understood; therefore, by these words not only their poverty, but also their chastity, is declared; and by the words, *"we have followed Thee,"* their obedience. The example of Jesus Christ was followed also by many of the first Christians.

I. They vowed *Poverty*, as may be proved from the example of Ananias and Saphira. These two had taken the vow of poverty. For in the Acts of the Apostles Chapt. V, 2, it is said, that by *fraud* they kept back part of the price of the land. Now fraud cannot be committed in things that are one's own, but only in things that belong to another. "The Apostle," says St. Augustine, "declares Ananias guilty of *fraud* and *sacrilege;* of sacrilege, because he deceived God in his promise; of *fraud,* because he kept back part of the goods which he had renounced by vow." Serm. 27.

Second—St. Peter accuses Ananias in the following manner: "Ananias, why hath Satan tempted thy heart, that thou shouldst lie to the Holy Ghost, and by fraud keep part of the price of the land?" Now had not Ananias vowed and promised poverty, he would have committed only an officious, not a pernicious lie about something that was his own. This would have been only a venial sin; just as if a man, giving a hundred dollars to a friend, would say: I would give more if I could. Peter becomes still more indignant, saying: "Why hast thou con-

1*

ceived this thing in thy heart?" i. e. a thing so impious, so sacrilegious! "Thou hast not lied to men, but to God." It is then evident that he had made to God the vow and promise of poverty; for no one is said to lie to God and to the Holy Ghost except he who does not keep what he promised by vow.

Third—That Ananias had vowed poverty, is also clear from his punishment. Peter punished him as well as his wife, by a sudden, public, and infamous death. Hence his sin must have been a grievous one, as it was in fact, being a sacrilegious violation of his vow.

II. Many of the first Christians vowed *Chastity*. This may be inferred from the circumstance, that those who gave what was of greater value, gave also what was of less value. Now it is something greater to renounce all the goods necessary for the present life, than to renounce marriage; for many renounce the latter merely to remain free from the troubles and crosses of that state.

Second—From the fervor of the first Christians, we may also infer that many of them vowed chastity. They were replenished with the Holy Ghost. According to St. Luke, "they were persevering in the doctrine of the Apostles." Act. II, 42. This doctrine was complete. It contained not only the precepts of Christ, but also His counsels, especially the following: "There are eunuchs who made themselves eunuchs for the Kingdom of Heaven. He that can take, let him take it." Matth. XIX, 12. To what else but the vow of chastity does this refer?

Third—Moreover, St. Luke says of the first Christians, that "they were persevering in the communication of the breaking of bread, and in prayer," Acts. II, 42, and verse 46 "and continuing daily with one accord in the temple, and breaking bread from house to house." If they received holy communion daily, and were all the time praying in the temple, we must needs conclude, that they were chaste. For this is the precept of St. Paul. I. Cor. VII, 5.

Fourth—The Corinthians, seeing that the first Christians of Jerusalem led a single life, commenced to doubt whether all Christians were not bound to do the same; hence it was, that they proposed this doubt to St. Paul who answered them, that celibacy was no precept, but only a counsel of the Lord. I. Cor. VII.

Fifth—The Essenians, at Alexandria, too, made the vow of chastity. They learned this from St. Mark, who instructed them, and who had observed that this was the life of the Christians of Jerusalem, who had been instructed by St. Peter, as is related by St. Jerome.*)

---

*) De Script. Eccles. in Marco.

III. They vowed *Obedience*. That many of the first Christians vowed obedience to the Apostles is evident from the arguments which prove their poverty and chastity; it is also evident from the fact that they brought the price of the things they sold, and laid it down together with their own persons. at the feet of the Apostles. , Act. IV, 35

In these first Christians, God wished to set an example for the Christians of all coming ages. In them he wished to give us models of a perfect Christian life which we should have before our eyes and try to imitate.

These Christians, then, led a religious life, and were true religious, as St. Jerome teaches.*) Cassian also **) teaches that the Institute of the Cenobites, or of those who lived in community, was established at the time of the Apostles. There were many in those days who, being very desirous of perfection, wished to do more than all the rest, and who, on that account, retired to secluded and little frequented places, where removed from the troubles of married and family life, and from intercourse with the world, they could more easily give themselves up to the contemplation of things and gifts more sublime. *From living in solitude*, they were called *monachi* (monks), and from living in com-

---

*) De Scrlpt. Eccles. in Philone.
**) Lib. 2—de Inst. Renunt. C. 5, et collat. 18, C. 5.)

munity, *coenobitae* (conobites). Their founders and principal teachers were St. Mark, the Evangelist, in Egypt; St. Matthew, in Aethiopia, where in a convent, he consecrated to the service of God, Iphigenia, the king's daughter, together with her companions; St. Paul, in Greece, where he consecrated to God St. Thecla; St. Clement at Rome, where he admitted St. Flavia Domitilla to the religious life; St. Martha, in Gaul, where she erected a convent, in which she and her companions consecrated themselves to God's service and led a celestial life.

That the religious life was instituted by the Apostles is affirmed by St. Dionysius who *) gives a description of the rites in use at the time of the Apostles for consecrating such persons to the service of God. We learn the same thing from St. John Chrysostom **), St. Augustine, Eusebius, and others.

About the Essenians, Eusebius, quoting the words of Philo, a learned Jew, who lived in the times of the Apostles, writes as follows: "No passion disturbs their minds; they enjoy the true liberty of men; no one possesses anything as his own, neither house, nor cattle, nor furniture; they have all things in common, and live together in com-

---

Eccles. Hierarch. c. 20.　**) Lib. 3, contra rituss vitae monast.

munity. Doing every thing for the good of the community, they have no preference for this or that occupation, but discharge their duties most cheerfully, regardless of cold, and heat, and change of weather. Some of them till the ground, others have charge of the cattle, others of the bees, and others again teach different arts and sciences. The wages which they receive for their labor they give to the Procurator of the Convent, who provides for them, and supplies them with all they need. They need, however, but very little, despising and holding in execration every thing that savors of luxury, which they consider to be the cause of bodily and spiritual sickness. None of them are servants, but all being quite free, serve one another. They approve only of that part of philosophy which treats of God and the creation of all things. They keep a strict watch over good morals. On the seventh day they betake themselves to the holy places where the sacred mysteries are performed; there they sit down in good order to listen to the reading and explanation of the Holy Scriptures. Thus they learn to lead a life of piety, holiness, and righteousness, applying themselves chiefly to three things, to a most ardent love of God, to a most assiduous practice of virtue, and to a most fervent charity towards their neighbor. There are many arguments to show that they love God most ardently: they always keep chastity; they never curse and swear, they hate lying, and especially do they believe that God is the author of all good things and of nothing bad.

That they are given up to the practice of virtue, is clear from the fact that they do not care for money, despise honors, hate sensual pleasures, and are always of an even and generous mind.

Their ardent love of God is also shown by their charity towards their neighbor, their benevolence, their sociableness, and their love for everything in common. No one amongst them lives in a house, which is not at the same time common to all; their income as well as their expenses are shared in common; and so is their clothing, their food, their drink, their meals and their whole life."

Hence St. Jerome * writes that the life of the primitive Christians was such as the monks of the present time endeavor to lead This manner of life was restored after the third century, by St. Anthony in Egypt; by St. Basil in Greece; by St. Jerome in Syria; by St. Augustine in Africa; by St. Benedict in Italy and the whole of the West. The latter was followed afterwards by St. Bernard, St. Dominic, St. Francis, St. Ignatius, St. Alphonsus and many others.

---

* Lib. in Philone.

Astonishing, indeed, is the number of those who have embraced the religious life in all ages of Christianity. St. Athanasius writes that in his time there were monasteries like Tabernacles, full of heavenly choirs of people, who spent their time in singing psalms, in reading and praying ; that they occupied a large extent of land and made, as it were, a town among themselves. Such immense numbers resorted to the religious life in Palestine, that Isidore was the Superior of one thousand monks, and his successor, Apollonius, of five thousand in the same monastery. In the cloistered community of Oryrynchus were ten thousand monks. Upon a hill in Nitria, about twenty miles from Alexandria, there were five hundred monasteries under one Superior. Palladins relates, that he saw a city in which there were more monasteries than houses of seculars ; "so that every street and corner, ringing with the divine praises, the whole city seemed a church." He also testifies to having seen multitudes of monks in Memphis and Babylon, and that not far from Thebes he met with a Father of three thousand monks. St. Pachomius who lived about three hundred years after Christ, had seven thousand disciples, besides one thousand in his own house ; and Serapion had ten thousand monks under his jurisdiction.

Theodoret records that there were also multitudes

of religious women throughout the East, in Palestine, Egypt, Asia, Pontus, Cilicia, Syria, and also in Europe. "Since our Saviour," he says, "was born of a Virgin Mother, the fields of holy virgins are everywhere multiplied."

Nor was the great increase of religious houses confined to the early ages of the church; for Trithemius (who died about the year 1516) says, that, in his time, the province of Ments alone contained one hundred and twenty-four Abbeys, and that there was a time when they had fifteen thousand Abbeys, besides Priories and other small monasteries belonging to his Order.

St. Bernard, in his life of St. Malachy, records that in Ireland there was a monastery, out of which many thousands of monks had come forth; "a holy place indeed," he says, "and fruitful in saints, bringing forth abundant fruit to God, in so much that one man alone of that holy congregation, whose name was Luanns, is reported to have been the founder of one hundred monasteries. And these swarms of saints have not only spread themselves in Ireland and Scotland, but have also gone into foreign parts; for St. Columba, coming from thence into France, built the monastery of Luxovium, and raised there a great people, their number being so great that the Divine praises were sung by them day and night without intermission. St. Columba

2

founded one hundred monasteries of which thirty-seven were in Ireland, a country which was for centuries known all over Europe as the Island of Saints and of Doctors.   According to Archdall there were in Ireland seven hundred and forty-two religious houses.

St. Bernard in the space of thirty years that he was Abbot, founded one hundred and sixty monasteries.   So rapid was the progress of his Order, that, in the space of fifty years from its establishment, it had acquired five hundred Abbeys and at one time no fewer than eight hundred were dependent on Clairvaux.

The Franciscans seem to have been particularly blessed in the speedy and extensive propagation of their Order; for, about the year 1600, one branch of this Order, called the Observantines, is said to have numbered one hundred thousand members. This Order reckons at present two hundred thousand men and three hundred thousand sisters including the Tertiaries.   It possesses two hundred and fifty-two provinces and twenty-six thousand convents, of which five are in Palestine and over thirty in Turkey.   More than eighty-nine emperors, kings and queens have been admitted into the order, which has moreover the glory of having furnished three thousand saints, or beatified persons, of whom seventeen hundred are martyrs.

Nor has the increase of all other male and female religious Orders and Congregations been less rapid and less wonderful in our days. What St. Athanasius says of religious societies of his time is applicable even in our own days: "Who is there," the saint exclaims, "that on beholding such a world of monks, that heroic company of people, continually striving after holiness of life, would not presently break forth into these words : How goodly are thy houses, O Jacob, and thy Tabernacles, O Israel? as woods that give shadow, as a garden upon rivers, as tents pitched by God, as cedars of Lebanon near the waters?" But what is most wonderful is that among this immense army of religious men and women, we behold so many Kings, Princes, the Nobility of both sexes, and men who have united eminent learning with great holiness of life.

In England, eleven Kings, from Sigebert to Egbert, exchanged the crown for the cowl. Indeed, it is recorded that thirty-two Kings of the Heptarchy, conscious of the impossibility of serving two masters —God and Mammon—resigned their crowns, and sold all, in order to feed the poor or build houses in honor of the Almighty.

The holy contention which took place between two sons of a British King about the year 657 is memorable. The elder brother on succeeding to the throne, disclosed to the other his design of

entering into Religion. He desired him at the same
time to prepare himself for the government of the
kingdom which he would soon leave to him.   The
younger brother requested to be allowed eight days
for consideration. In the meantime he betook himself privately to a monastery, thinking within himself if it were best for his brother to forsake the
government, it could not be good for him to accept it.

Among the women of noble blood who joined the
Order of St. Francis, professing the poverty of St.
Clara, are Sancha, Queen of Sicily in the year 1340;
Agnes, daughter to a King of Bohemia about the
year 1240; for though given in marriage to
Frederick II., she would never yield her consent,
but vowed virginity in a monastery in Prague; a
daughter of the King of Hungary, who though
espoused to Boleslaus, surnamed *The Chaste*, King
of Poland, kept her virginity with him, and afterwards led a religious life in a monastery founded by
herself; Joan, daughter of the King of Navarre;
Isabel, sister to St. Louis; Blanche, daughter of
Philip, King of France; Margaret, of Austria,
daughter of the Emperor Maximilian; and Marie,
sister to King Philip, of Spain. About 1770, Louisa,
daughter of Louis XV., King of France, entered a
Convent of Carmelite nuns. Amongst the Abbesses
of the Order of Fontevrault, founded by Robert of
Abrisseh, who lived to see three thousand nuns in

one house of his Order, are counted fourteen princesses of whom five were of the royal house of Bourbon.

St. Bernard, then, could write in truth to a company of young noblemen who had joined his (the Cistercian) Order : "I have read," he writes, "that God chose not many noblemen, not many wise men, not many powerful; but now by the wonderful power of God, contrary to the ordinary course, a multitude of such people is converted. The glory of this present life becomes contemptible, the flower of youth is trodden under foot, nobility not regarded, the wisdom of the world accounted folly, flesh and blood rejected, the affection of friends and kinsfolk renounced ; favor, honor, dignity esteemed as dirt, that Christ may be gained." Thus is verified what the Lord foretold by the Prophet Zacharias: "In those days, it will come to pass that ten men of all languages shall take hold, and shall hold fast the habit of one of My servants, saying : we will go with you: for we have heard that the Lord is with you."

But to enumerate all those religious men who have been eminent in learning and sanctity and have embraced the religious life, would occupy too much space ; I must therefore confine myself to a few only who have joined exquisite learning to singular virtue. Amongst these, Serapion appears in the

2*

first age, about 193. He was Bishop of Antioch and the eighth in order after St. Peter the Apostle. He was looked upon as the most learned and most eloquent man of his time. Pamphilius and Lucian, about 311, and John Climachus, in 550, were monks. The writings of St. Basil and St. Gregory Nazianzen are well known; St. Epiphanius was also a learned and holy man, and so was particularly St. John Chrysostom, who flurished about 400. St. John Damascene, whose works also are extant, was very famous about 754. St. Athanasius, Bessarion and many other great men in the East, were also monks.

Among the Latins, those two great lights of the Church, St. Jerome and St. Augustine, claim the first place, as being amongst the most eloquent, learned and holy Doctors of the Church. That great man, St. Martin of Tours, was also a monk, and so were St. John Cassian, Eucherius, Bishop of Lyons; St. Prosper, St. Fulgentius, St. Gregory the Great, St. Gregory of Tours, St. Isidore, St. Ildefonsus, St. Thomas Aquinas, St. Bonaventure and Venerable Bede in England. St. Anselm was at first a monk, and afterwards Archbishop of Canterbury, and St. Alphonsus Liguori was a monk and founder of a Religious Order. In short, out of the four Greek Doctors three were religious; of the Latin Doctors, also three.

In fact, many Holy Pontiffs, through the love of

peace, and solitude, and cloistral life, renounced their bishopricks, following the example of St. Gregory Nazianzen, St. Justus, Archbishop of Lyons, St. Vulfran, Bishop of Sens, and Pope Celestine V., John, the predecessor of the great Gerbert, in the see of Ravenna, had withdrawn into wilderness of the mountains of Capareo. In 1267, Isaac O'Gorman, Bishop of Killaloe, resigned that see and became a monk in the abbey of the Holy Cross. To Monte-Cassino, came the holy Bishop Bruno, wishing to serve God with more freedom under the monastic habit in that monastery, far from the tumult of the world.

In the eleventh century, Bertrand, Bishop of Frejus, renounced his see, and retired to the abbey of Lerins, where he died in the odor of sanctity.

Walter Mauclerc, Chancellor of England, in the reign of Henry III., and bishop of Carlisle, took refuge in the order of St. Dominic, abandoning all things, even to his cloak, as Matthew of Paris says, when he entered the monastery of Oxford. The abbey of Medard at Soissons was chosen by many great prelates for their place of rest, after abdicating their sees, numbers of whom were buried beneath its vaults.

Many prelates retired to monasteries expressly to die. Cardinal George d'Amboise came with this intention to the monastery of the Celestins at Lyons. Comparing his own life with that of the monk, brother John, who waited on him in his sickness, he often said to him: "Ah, brother John, my friend, would that I had been brother John."

To show the great love and esteem of the prelates of the church for religious orders, it was the custom in the twelfth century, when a bishop died, to carry his body about from monastery to monastery, leaving it a day and night in each, till the whole number of religious houses in the diocese had been visited. This usage was observed, for instance, at the funeral of Adalbert, Archbishop of Treves.

All these learned and holy men, by the contempt of glory, have been more gloriously exalted, and more sublimely glorified. Of each of them is true what St. Augustine said of himself. "I have," he writes, "been much in love with the perfection of which our Saviour, speaking to the young man, said: 'Go and sell all thou hast and give to the poor, and come, follow Me;' and not by my own strength, but by the help of the grace of God have I performed it, and know more than any other, how much I have profited in this way of perfection; yet God knows it better than I do. And I exhort others all I can to the same course of life, and I have companions in it, who have been persuaded by my reasons." Assuredly, to find such a number of persons, eminent for wisdom, piety and learning, forsaking all worldly possessions and embracing the religious life, must be one of its best commendations

CHAPTER III.

THE principal end of every religious Order and Congregation is the sanctification of its members. The Catholic Church, the promoter of perfection, the fruitful parent of virginity, sanctions the establishment of Religious Orders and protects them by her decrees, to give a home to such of her children as, being zealous of the better gifts, are not content with the observance of the commandments, but aspire to the perfection of the counsels. The chief business or end of all Religious, then, is to strive to attain perfection. For this they are separated totally, but honorably, from the world; for this they have quitted happy homes and affectionate friends: "The Lord thy God hath chosen thee to be His peculiar people, and to make thee higher than all the nations. He hath made thee to His own praise, Name and Glory." To reach this end they take the three religious vows of Poverty, Chastity and Obedience.

It is Religious that should prove to the world
that the Gospel counsels are not impracticable
Their piety should make reparation for the ingratitude of sinful, thoughtless man ; their virtues should
impetrate graces for the universe.　Wherever they
reside, they ought to be as the ten just men for
whose sake God promised to spare the sinful city.
Whether they follow the austere rule of St. Bruno
with the Carthusians, or the mild rule of St.
Augustine with the Ursulines, Visitandines and
Sisters of Mercy, their chief duty is to attain to the
perfection to which they are called.　This end is
common to all.

Besides this end, they have a secondary end,
which is the advancement of the salvation of their
neighbor. It is this secondary end which distinguish-
es all religious societies one from another. To reach
this end, their life is either contemplative, active,
or mixed.

It is *contemplative* when spent exclusively in
contemplation, prayer, and spiritual exercises tending directly to the love of, and to union with, God.
Such is the life of the monks of St. Anthony, St.
Basil, St. Benedict, St. Romuald, St. Bruno and
others.　A spirit of retirement, or a love of holy
solitude and its exercises, and an habitual interior
recollection are essential to piety and a true Christian
life.　Some, by a particular call of God, dedicate

themselves to His service in a state of perfect solitude, in which the first motive may be self-defence or preservation. In the world snares are laid everywhere for us, and its lusts often endeavor to court and betray us, and the torrent of its example or the violence of its persecution to drive and force us unto death. Whoever therefore prudently fears that he is not a match for so potent an enemy, may, nay sometimes ought, to retire from the world. This is not to decline the service of God or man, but to fly from sin and danger; it is not to prefer ease and security to industry and labor, but to rash presumption and a fatal overthrow. But entire solitude is a safer state only to those who are animated with such a love and esteem for all its exercises as give an assurance of their constant fervor in them; who also seriously cultivate interior solitude of mind, and will never suffer it to seek after the objects of worldly affairs, vanities, or pleasures; whose souls, lastly, are free from envy, emulation, ambition, desire of esteem, and all other busy and turbulent passions, which cannot fail by desires and hankerings to discompose the mind, to disturb the pure stream, and adulterate the relish for a retired life. The soul must be reduced to its native purity and simplicity before it will be able to taste the blessings of true liberty, of regular devotion and elevated meditation. An indication that God designs certain persons for retirement is the discovery of talents fitted for this state rather than for any public station. For there are active and contemplative gifts. Those who are destined by heaven to a retired life, in it become most eminently serviceable to the world by proving excellent examples of innocence, and the perfect spirit of every Christian virtue, and by their prayers and continual pure homages of praise and thanksgivings to God, from which others may reap far more valuable benefits than from the labors of the learned, or the bountiful alms of the rich. Thus the world never loses a member, but has the benefit of his service in its proper place, and in the most effectual manner. This sort of life contributes towards the salvation of our neighbor in the same manner in which Moses, by his prayer, contributed towards the victory which the Jews gained over their enemies.

By *active* life is unterstood that which is solely occupied with external works of charity; this manner of life, too, tends principally and ultimately to the love of God, but only in a indirect manner. Such is the life of the Knights of Jerusalem, of St. James, St. John and of the Brothers of the Redemption, of Christians in captivity.

By the *mixed* life is understood that which unites both the contemplative and active, and tends to the love both of God and our neighbor. Such is the life of the Orders of St. Augustine, St. Dominic, St. Francis, St. Ignatius, St. Alphonsus and others.

The mixed life is considered to be the most perfect. St. Thomas teaches us that, though the contemplative life in itself is more perfect than the active, yet the mixed life is the most perfect of all, for it was the life of Jesus Christ Himself. "As it is something greater to enlighten than to shine," says St. Thomas, "so, in like manner, it is something greater to communicate to others the fruits of contemplation than merely to contemplate." When Elias retired into the desert, the Lord made him the following reproach: "What are you doing?" just as if the Lord said to him : There is no time now to give yourself up to a life of quiet contemplation. Our Lord Jesus Christ, too, deferred His ascension into heaven for forty days, in order to instruct His disciples. St. Francis believed that he would please God better if, from time to time, he should leave contemplation alone and go out to preach to the people.

This secondary end, then, refers to the duties which Religious freely contract towards their neighbor, and which are specified in their rules.

Now, this secondary end is always just what the Church wants most at the epoch in which each Order or Congregation makes its appearance. Almighty God, Who incessantly watches over the welfare of

3

His church, has, in every century, provided chosen vessels —saints —to defend and edify her and to supply her wants. And such saints —in themselves alone magnificent gifts of Providence,—are invariably endowed by Heaven with the graces peculiarly necessary, at that precise moment, for the healing of the world and the victory of the Church.

Aga nst Aranism, God raised up an Athanasius and a Hilary of Poitiers ; to oppose the Nestorians, God sent St. Cyril. ' He sent St. Augustine to beat down the Pelagians ; St. John Damascene to fight the Iconoclasts. In the decline of the Roman Empire, and to counteract the vices of the decadence, God sent St. Benedict and his legion of toiling monks. When the world became Christian, and Catholics grew rich and forgot the poverty of our Lord Jesus Christ, St. Francis was called to teach the love of Christian poverty to voluptuous Catholics.

Heresy and ignorance then followed, and St. Dominic was raised up by God to combat these two great evils ; and therefore the vocation of the Dominicans is to teach and to preach. In the sixteenth century, Protestantism came up. Heresy arose in all its strength—Luther was its ring-leader and its spokesman, sensual passion and disobedience were personified in him. God raised up St. Ignatius and in him the Society of Jesus to oppose Protestantism by self-denial, by an especial vow to the

Holy See, and by their sound teachings of the Catholic Religion.

Finally, in the eighteenth century, infidelity and impiety, the last consequences of Protestantism, personified in Voltaire and his associates, boldly raised their heads. Infidelity naturally united with Jansenism and Rigorism to undermine the edifice of the Church. Rigorism took hold of confessors and armed them with iron sternness against weak and shuddering sinners. The consequence was that servile fear took the place of the charity of God; that the sacraments, the fountains of life, were abandoned, or turned into derision; that the Blessed Eucharist, the life-spring of Catholic piety, became an object of dread, and that the spirit of Christianity seemed to pass away. But the eye of an omniscient Providence was watching over it. In order to confound impiety and infidelity, to fight against Jansenism, to disarm confessors of their overstrained rigidity, to awaken faith, to kindle in the hearts of the faithful love for the Blessed Sacrament, God gave to His church a man after His own heart, Alphonsus de Liguori. Infidelity had permeated society from the nobility to the lower classes, and the sons of St. Alphonsus, the Redemptorist Fathers, are preaching to the poor the eternal truths which they may have lost sight of by indifferentism and infidelity.

God gave St. Vincent de Paul to succor the poor,

De la Salle to educate poor boys, Nano Nagle to educate poor girls; and when the fierce Revolution had swept away all vestiges of the Catholic schools of France, the venerated Madame Barat established, for the education of the rich and the poor, the admirable Society of the Sacred Heart. The same Providence that gave these illustrious personages to His Church and His people, raised up in our days Catharine McAuley, just before the awful times of cholera and famine and godless education, to found the Order of Mercy, for the special relief of the poor in their numerous and ever-varying exigencies. As in the church of God there are religious to serve in the hospitals and take particular care of the body in illness, so, in the same manner, it is very necessary that there should be religious, who receive into their convents souls that are ill, in order to restore them to spiritual health. And as there are Ursuline Religious, whose principal object is to employ themselves in forming innocent souls to the fear of God, so, in like manner, it is very important that there should be others, whose particular object is to labor to re-establish this same fear in penitent souls. For the accomplishment of this object, our Lord called into existence the Sisters of the Good Shepherd, who have so wonderfully increased that the late Mother Superior General founded one hundred and ten houses.

Truly God never made use of better instruments in the furtherance of His benevolent designs in regard to fallen man, than the male and female members of Religious Orders, and the latter more especially in our days. These spotless virgins have devoted themselves to the blessed functions of instructing the ignorant, the poor, the needy, the orphan, the houseless, the forlorn, the despised as well as the more favored of the earth, to soothing the sufferings of the sick, to works of charity and mercy, to prayer, meditation and self-denial. They are the glory and ornament of the Church and the gentle disciples of her whose immaculate purity made her worthy to bear, in her chaste womb, the Incarnate Son of the Most High; they are especially privileged "to follow the Lamb whithersoever He goeth." Estranged from the world and its false allurements, their delight is to do the will of God. For this reason, they are always joyous and happy, and proficients in the practice of self-denial, meekness, humility, and the other virtues. They make no grandiloquent printed reports, in costly binding; they have no official stenographers or reporters to noise their proceedings in "morning papers;" they have no "Polytechnic Halls," fitted up with pretentious libraries, and all the surroundings of upholstery, and heating and cooling apparatus; but winter and summer, early and late, they keep the even tenor of

3*

their way with an *"eye single"* to their humble and
laborious duties.

In nearly all the cities of America, in those busy
and worldly centres of traffic and trade, of luxury
and wealth, with their average of good and evil,
virtue and crime, this *"volunteer army"* distributes
itself noiselessly, quietly, and as it were, obscurely,
not heralded nor preceded by the emblems of pomp
or worldly power, but nevertheless making its con-
quests and asserting its quiet influence in lanes and
alleys, gathering up the little children, taking them
to its camps, and instructing and educating them
in the service of God and society.

My dear reader, you may have seen, in some of
those cities, that long line of little boys or girls—
two by two, extending to the length of a block or
more ; you may have observed how regularly they
are assorted, the tallest in first, and ranging down
to the little ones, whose busy feet are trying to keep
up with the column.   You may also have noted the
order and silence (so unusual among children) and
your attention was arrested, and perhaps you know
not how all this order in this beautiful panorama
was brought about.   Well, with these boys you
may have observed two men, one at the head, the
other at the foot of this long line.   If you saw this
for the first time, you may have wondered, and I
suppose, been even amused, at the figure and cos-

tume of those men—the broad-brimmed hat, the long, strange-fashioned robe, the white collar, the collected air and mien, all bespeak the *Christian Brother*. These men, nevertheless, are "profoundly learned in all the sciences of the schools." They have abandoned home, family, friends, and have devoted themselves, merely for a scant support, to the education of the young.

If, on the other hand, the long line are girls, you may have observed two ladies, one at the head, the other at the foot. You will at a glance conclude they are not of the world. Their costume is of the homeliest cut and quality, but scrupulously clean; there is a something about their very presence that impresses you with reverence and respect, and you must be a very hardened sinner, indeed, if you did not feel the better of having even their shadow fall upon you. These silent, collected, but impressive women are "Nuns" of one order or another. They, too, have left all to serve God in the persons of these little children. They have made sacrifices greater than the world can appreciate or understand, and which only the Divine Master can reward. Their whole life is a silent, but an eloquent sermon, their whole conduct the gospel in action. You will remember, they are women like others of their sex, and may have been flattered and petted, and once filled with the natural vanity and expectations of their sex; but all these they have put *behind* them, and henceforth and forever their walk and life and conversation is with God, and in the service of His little ones. Now, it will be easily seen that the personal influence of such men and women over the life and manners of children must be immensely beneficial. It is granted that the influence of father and mother is potential for good or evil. So it is with teachers. Children are shrewd observers, and are apt to take some one as a prototype and exemplar. This one they copy as near as may be. These "Christian Brothers" and "Nuns or Sisters" are good copies; they teach the children to pray in the best of all ways,—by praying themselves first; they try to impress on these tender souls sentiments of love, obedience and respect to their fathers and mothers, and above all their duties to our dear Lord. They accompany them to His altar on Sundays and holy days, beginning and ending all their daily lessons with a little prayer or devotion. For the rest they teach them in their schools all the branches of literature and science.

The Editor of the *New York Herald* prefaces an account of a Catholic Academy with the following remarks:. "However divided public opinion may be as to secular and religious schools—no matter what differences in opinion may exist in the community as to the policy of aiding or discouraging purely sectarian systems of education—there can be but little opposition from any quarter to the verdict of experience given by many thousand families, that these devoted women, the Sisters of the Catholic Church, are the best teachers of young girls, the safest instructors in this age of loose, worldly and rampant New Englandism. Those matters of education which make the lady in their hands subordinate to the great object of making every girl committed to their care a true woman imbued with those principles which have made our mothers our pride and boast. Those of us who cavil at Catholic pretentions, sneer at their assumption, and ridicule their observances, must acknowledge that the Sisters are far ahead and above any organization of the sort of which Protestantism can boast. The self-sacrifice, the devotion, the single-mindedness, the calm trust in a power unseen, the humility of manner and rare unselfishness which characterize the Sisters, has no parallel in any organization of the reformed faith. The war placed the claims of the Sisters of Charity fairly before the country, but these Sisters of the different branches have in peace ' victories no less renowned than in war.' Educating the poor children, directing the untutored mind of the youthful alien savage in our midst, or holding the beacon of intellectual advancement bright and burning before the female youth of the country, and beckoning them to advance, they are ever doing a good and noble work."

Just, then, as a good General, when the battle is begun, observes from a rising ground the state of the combat, in order to send reinforcements wherever they are wanted, so also Jesus Christ Who is the General of the Christian army, beholds from the heavens above the state of His Church in the different combats which she has to sustain, and according to her necessities, He sends from time to time, new reinforcements of doctors and heads of Orders to succor her; and herein the Providence and Mercy of our Saviour is very great, never permitting any distemper without applying a remedy in due time.

It is, then, in this secondary end that the religious Orders and Congregations differ from one another. Those Orders which are exclusively contemplative, are, as I have already remarked, distinguished from those which lead an active or mixed life, by promoting not *directly*, but rather *indirectly* the salvation of their neighbors, by means of their prayers, fasting and of the other good works which they perform and offer up for this end. Religious Orders or Congregations professing the active or mixed life are distinguished from one another in this, that none of them embraces every kind of labor and good work tending to afford spiritual or corporal aid to their fellow-men, but each one is restricted to a certain kind specified by their rule.

Every founder of a religious society professing the mixed life, had in view an institute whose members should not only imitate the virtues and examples of our Divine Saviour, but should also imitate, as perfectly as human frailty will permit, His manner of acting and living in this world. For just as our Lord and Redeemer was wont to withdraw from the society of men at certain times, and go forth to preach the word of salvation, convert sinners, and preach the Gospel to the poor especially, so, in like manner, did the founders of these religious Orders and Congregations wish that the members thereof should at one time be employed at home in prayer and the exercise of piety, devotion and every virtue; and at another, go out to exercise such functions of the ministry or charity, as the secondary ends of their respective Institutes required.

To give an example: The chief labors of the Society of Jesus consist in giving Missions and spiritual exercises, in preaching the Divine Word, in hearing confessions, in the direction of seminaries and colleges, and in educating young men. In the Congregation of the Most Holy Redeemer, the chief labors also consist in giving Missions and spiritual exercises, in preaching, in instructing the ignorant, and hearing confessions; but the ordinary care of souls, the direction of seminaries, education of youth and the like, are excluded from this Institute as being labors which, although they aim at promoting the interests of faith and piety, and the salvation of souls, are foreign to its specific end, and would prevent its members from prosecuting that end with all their strength. Moreover, although the Apostolic ministry, by its very nature, regards every sex, age and condition, as also all classes of human society, to the exclusion of none, yet, according to the views with which Heaven inspired St. Alphonsus, the Founder of this Congregation, and by the prescription of its rule, its members are bound to make it their special care to assist the poor and destitute and to prefer them, and, in general, men of inferior condition,—in as far as they have the choice—to those occupying a higher station of life.

We may then say, that the difference of religious Orders arises from the difference of the dispositions of man; for what pleases one would not be grateful to another; what would benefit one would injure another. Some like solitude, others society; one loves contemplation, another action. It was for this reason that the holy Fathers instituted so many different modes of life as conducive to salvation and suiting the divisions of graces, of ministrations, and of works which were inspired by the same divine Spirit. Of divers voices is sweet music made, and so in the Church different Orders render sweet harmony; for all are so arranged that none could see and not admire them. Therefore, Pope Clement IV. replied to a knight who asked which Order he ought to embrace, "They all tend to the same end, which is the salvation of souls; whether you embrace this rule or that, you will take the narrow way and enter by the gate into the land of milk and honey. Examine, then, carefully which Order is most suitable to your genius, and adhere to it, so as not to withdraw your love from others;" for "some," says St. Bonaventure, "tend to God by quiet, others by labor; some in this manner, others in that; and often what is esteemed the least is the best. Therefore, do not judge any one to be more imperfect than yourself, because he does not perform all the things which you do " (Stim. Amoris, P. III. c. 9.) Holy is the Order of the Franciscans, holy the Order of the Dominicans, holy the Order of the Jesuits, of the Redemptorists etc., in all of them the Lord has placed the ministry of reconciliation, and the way of safety.

Hence "religious on a journey," as St. Bonaventure writes, "are carefully to avoid exalting the merit and excellence of their own Order, dwelling on the detail of its advantages, so as to praise it to the disparagement of other Institutes; they are to esteem it without making any invidious comparisons; for it is wickedness to praise one's self while depreciat-

2

ing others." (Spec. Novit. c. 32.) "Heaven forbid that any one should believe God to be local," says a monk of Cluny, writing for the instruction of an abbot of a monastery at Spires, "so as to suppose that He cannot perform in the territory of Spires what He does in Francy. Only let His mercy be with you that He Who proves the reins and the heart may see that His precepts are observed with the same simplicity and with no less regard to His will. What does it matter whether one is instructed by the example of a Franciscan, or of a Jesuit, or a Redemptorist? Once baptized, there is no Order in the whole church of God in which a good man cannot be saved, and in which a bad man will not be condemned: so that whether you take the habit of St. Francis, or of St. Ignatius, or of St. Alphonsus de Liguori, or of any other, it matters little, since they are all holy habits, instituted by holy men. "I am a Cistercian," says St. Bernard; "do I therefore condemn the Clumiacs? God forbid; but I love them, but I magnify them. Why then, you will say, did I not embrace the Order? Because each one has his particular calling, and all things are not expedient; and different medicines are required for different diseases. I praise and love all Orders, wherever there is a pious and holy life in the church. *Unum opere teneo; ceteros, charitate.* In fine let it be remembered, that whatever may be our observance, those who live orderly, and yet speak proudly, make themselves citizens of Babylon, and sons of darkness and of hell, where is nor order, but eternal horror dwelleth."

"There was a strife amongst them which of them should seem to be greater." (Luke 22, 24.) This root of dissension was taken away by our Lord saying: "He who is the greatest among you, let him be your servant." Who, after this, will say: "*Ego melior sum,* I am better."? If any one asks me who is best? If I am a Canon, I answer: The monks are best; if I am a monk my reply is, The Canons are best. This is the rule of a Christian.

Every religious, as St. Francis de Sales excellently observes, should reverence and esteem the Orders which labor for the glory of God, the edification of the Church, the salvation of souls; he should be hostile to none; he should endeavor to rival none, except in the greater love of Jesus and Mary; nay, looking upon his own as the least of all, he should readily yield to others the first place of dignity and honor; yet he should bestow his sentiments of peculiar love, tenderness and filial affection on his own Order, as being that living ark of salvation, which God has prepared for him from all eternity, to save him from the deluge and corruption of the world.

Hence every religious is bound to love his Order

with the greatest possible affection, as the mother that brought him forth spiritually, and who after having thus brought him forth, does not cease to nourish him with spiritual milk. Nothing should be dearer to him in this world than the welfare of this mother; he should be ever ready for any sacrifice for her temporal or spiritual good; rejoicing with her when she rejoices, and weeping with her when she weeps; he should make her consolations and affections his own; he should regard with a filial eye and bear with a filial heart the imperfections, blemishes, and all the miseries from which, according to the divine saying : "It must be that scandals come." No Religious Institute is found to be exempt. He should not, however, on this account neglect to fulfill his duties, but, on the contrary, he should strive, with all his might, by words and deeds, and by his example, to uphold regular observance, fervor, and the true spirit of his holy Founder, upon the maintenance of which alone depends the true welfare of the Order, its increase and the blessing of God upon it.   If any one should lack these sentiments of love and affection, he would not, indeed, fail directly against the vows of Poverty, Chastity and Obedience, but he would incur the reproach which the Apostle made to the heathens, viz : that they were without affection. (Rom 1, 31.) Nay, he would show such ingratitude towards God for the grace of vocation, as scarcely to justify the hope of being tolerated by the Lord in His holy house. "For the hope of the unthankful shall melt away as the winter's ice and shall run off as unprofitable water." (Wisdom **16, 29.**)

CHAPTER IV.

"HE who shall leave his home, brothers, or sisters, or father, or mother, or wife, or children, or estate for My sake, shall receive a hundred-fold in this life, and eternal life hereafter in the world to come." Matt. 19, 29.

These words of our Lord have induced thousands of both sexes to despise and abandon the world and embrace the religious life. This promise of Jesus Christ has filled the Deserts with anchorites, and the cloisters with religious. Let us search diligently into the riches of this promise, let us acquaint ourselves thoroughly with the treasures which it contains.

Jesus Christ has promised to His followers the hundred-fold both of temporal and spiritual blessings. The Son of God knows that men are extremely self-interested; that they seem to have no courage to undertake anything unless they see some present advantage. It is for this reason that Jesus Christ does not wish that those who renounce all things for His sake, should go unrewarded even in this life. He does not wish that His followers should give Him a long credit, that is, much time to repay them for their generosity in renouncing the world with all its false and transitory pleasures. He therefore says: "He who shall leave his house, brothers or sisters, or father or mother, or wife or children, or estate for My sake shall receive a *hundred fold in this life.*

Now this promise is literally fulfilled. Leave one house only, that of your father, for the love of Jesus Christ, and in return for it, He gives you as many as the religious Order or Congregation of which you become a member may possess. Forsake your earthly father and God gives you many spiritual parents, who love you more tenderly, who are much more solicitous for your welfare, than your father according to the flesh could be.

Leave your brothers and sisters, and God gives you many others, whose love for you is far more sincere, because loving you as they do only in God and for God's sake, their love is free from self-interest whereas your brothers in the world hardly loved you for any other reason than self-interest.

Leave those who wait upon you in the world (if indeed you have any such to leave) and you will find many brethren in the convent, who are always employed in your service; one will serve you as steward, another as porter, another again as cook, or as infirmarian etc.

And what is more, should you be sent to other countries you will allways find a house of the Order or Congregation ready to receive you, and the same attendance to wait upon you. Now is this not to receive a hundred fold and more than a hundred fold in this life?

Leave all your riches and God gives you much more in religion. By leaving them, you are rendered master of them through His Grace, whilst those in the world who possess them, are rather their slaves than their owners, for they are constantly tormented by care and solicitude to increase and preserve them. "Their wealth," says Solomon, "even robs them of their sleep." Eccl. V., 11.

In religion, on the contrary, God lets you have every thing you want, without the trouble of knowing whether it be dear or cheap; you live, to use the words of St. Paul, "as having nothing, yet possessing all things." (II. Cor. VI., 10.)

As for ease of mind, you have a hundred times more in religion, than you would have had in the world. Do people in the world not readily avow that they are hourly exposed to a thousand misfortunes, disquietudes and troubles?

How great are not the misfortunes of so many married people. Even before their marriage, and when they marry, and even after marriage, all is trouble and vexation and full of a world of miseries; if they seem to have any trifling delight, it is nothing if compared with their griefs, because it is drowned in their present calamities, and in those which hang over them for the future. Their miseries are matter enough to make a tragedy. No one can conceive the world of miseries, to which married people are subject, unless he has tried them; they only who have made the experience truly know that there is far more sorrow and bitterness in the delights which people expect to enjoy, than pleasure and contentment. Riches, the shadows of honor and all other things of the same nature, wherein men think themselves happy, are void of true happiness. What comfort and peace can they give ? It is far more honorable not to stand in need of them than to possess them; the fear of loosing them torments man more than the burning desire of obtaining them.

A religious life is free from all these evils, vexations and miseries, which so much perplex people of the world, and actually tear their hearts to pieces. Let the life of a religious appear to the world ever so distasteful, it is certain that it is far sweeter and more desirable than any other kind of life, howsoever sweet and pleasing it may seem.

The Order or Congregation to which you belong

charges itself with the care of all the necessaries of life, in order that, being freed from all such anxiety and solicitude, you may enjoy constant peace of mind and tranquillity of heart, and be thus enabled continually to raise your thoughts towards heaven.

Again, suppose you desire to rise to high honor in this world. "I am," I hear you say, "noble creature and therefore it is natural for me to desire worldly honor and dignities." Well, you have them in greater abundance in your religious habit. Princes, Lords, Bishops and Magistrates, who perhaps would not have taken notice of you before, now pay you deference and respect on account of the habit which you wear, or the Order to which you belong. Thus the Lord returns, even in this life with usury, whatever you renounce in the world, for His sake.

But now, if we come to speak of the *spiritual advantages* of the religious life, we must avow that language is incapable of giving an adequate description of them. To religious we may well apply what St. John says of the inhabitants of heaven : "After this I saw a great multitude of all nations, and tribes, and people, and tongues, standing before the throne, and in the sight of the Lamb; they are come out of great tribulation, clothed with white robes; they have made them white in the blood of the Lamb, and with palms in their hands—and they serve Him day and night in His temple; and He that sitteth on the throne shall dwell over them. They shall no more hunger nor thirst. For the Lamb shall rule over them and lead them to the fountains of the waters of life, and God shall wipe away all their tears from their eyes. (Apoc. vii.)

1. Those who enter religion begin to lead a life quite celestial and angelic. Like the blessed spirits in heaven, *"they serve God in the Temple."* Religion, or the monastic life is a kind of heaven or Temple of God on earth.

"It is a terrestial Paradise," says St. Bernard, "made by the hand of God Himself, in order that man may lead in it a blissful life. Your profession is most sublime; it is higher than the heavens; it is equal to the angels; it resembles angelical purity, because you have vowed not only all kinds of sanctity, but also the perfection of all kind of sanctity— even the highest perfection. It is for others to serve God, but for you to be united to Him. What name, therefore, shall I give you that is worthy of you? Shall I call you heavenly men, or earthly angels? For though you live upon earth, your conversation and your thoughts are in heaven, for you are no longer strangers and pilgrims upon earth, but fellow-citizens of the Saints and domestics of God."

Religious persons constantly practise the virtue of religion, the noblest of all moral virtues, which teaches us to worship and serve God in a manner worthy of Him, and to refer all things to Him as to their true Author, and to offer our souls to Him pure and immaculate; for they have dedicated and consecrated themselves for ever to the divine ser- vice, and all they do is done from the vow of obe- dience, which is dictated by the virtue of religion, and to which they subject themselves from the sole motive of the love of God. Such as the tree is, such is the fruit. If the tree is consecrated to God, the fruit which it produces is so too. All religious persons are so many trees, as it were, consecrated to God and His service; hence all their actions, the fruits of these trees, are so many acts of religion, that is, holy sacrifices offered to Almighty God. To illustrate still better. A fast, which is an act of the virtue of temperance, becomes also an act of religion by vow which enhances its merit so as to attach to it, both the merit of the good act itself, which is temperance, and the merit of the acts of religion by reason of the vow. In like manner a religious acquires double merit in everything he does out of obedience, that is, he acquires the merit of the good action itself and that of obedience. Thus a religious lives more purely, says St. Bernard, all his actions being in themselves most pure and ac- ceptable before God, because they are in conformity to His will, and free from the corruption of self-will.

It is on this account that Gilbert, the Abbot, says (serm. 87) that the meanest work of a religious is more meritorious in the sight of God than the most heroic action of a secular person. "The actions of a secular," says St. Alphonsus, "however holy and fervent he may be, partake more of self-will than those of religious. Seculars pray, communicate, hear mass, read, take the discipline, and recite the divine office when they please. But a religious performs these duties at the time prescribed by obedience—that is, by the holy will of God. For, in his rule, and in the commands of his superior, he hears His voice. Hence, a religious who obeys his rule and his superior merits an eternal reward, not only by his prayers and by the performance of his spiritual duties, but also by his labors, his recreations, and attendance at the door; by his meals, his amusements, and his repose. For, since the performance of all these duties is dictated by obedionee, and not by self-will, he does in each the holy will of God, and by each he earns an everlasting crown of glory. Oh! how often does self-will vitiate the most holy actions! Alas! to how many, on the day of judgement, when they shall ask, in the words of Isaiah, the reward of their labors—·'Why have we fasted, and Thou hast not regarded? why have we humbled our souls, and Thou hast not taken notice?"—to how many, I say, will the Almighty

Judge answer—"Behold, in the day of your fast, your own will is found." What! He will say, do you demand a reward? Have you not, in doing your own will, already received the recompense of your toils? Have you not, in all your duties, in all your works of penance, sought the indulgence of your own inclinations, rather than the fulfilment of my will? St. Bernard asserts, that if a person in the world did the fourth part of what is ordinarily done by religious, he would be venerated as a Saint. And has not experience shown that the virtues of many, whose sanctity shone resplendent in the world, faded away before the bright examples of the fervent souls whom, on entering religion, they found in the cloister?

A religious then, because he has consecrated himself to God by vow and does in all his actions the holy will of God, can truely say, that he together with all his works belong entirely to the Lord, having nothing more left to give Him. Thus it is that, like the blessed of heaven, he is constantly serving the Lord in his holy state of religion, in *this Temple of God* and in *this Paradise on earth.*

2. The Blessed in heaven "are clothed with white robes; and they have made them white in the Blood of the Lamb." Religious, too, put on a white robe on the day of their profession, which is of so great a merit before God, that it satisfies His

justice, canceling as it does all their sins and punishments due to them. It is on this account that the
religious profession is called a second baptism by
the divines and the Fathers of the church. "It may
be reasonably said," says St. Thomas, "that a person by entering into religion, obtains the remission
of all sins. For, to make satisfaction for all sins,
it is sufficient to dedicate oneself entirely to the
service of God by entering religion, which dedica-
tion exceeds all manner of satisfaction. Hence we
read in the lives of the Fathers, that they who enter
into religion obtain the same graces as those who
receive baptism." (2. 29. ult. a. 3, ad 3.)

One day St. Anthony, the hermit, had a vision.
It seemed to him that he was carried up to heaven
by angels, but that many devils came and tried to
prevent them from proceeding further, saying that
Anthony had committed several sins in the world.
But the angels answered that if they had anything
to accuse him of, since he became a religious, they
might tell it; but as to the sins committed by him
in the world, they were already pardoned by reason
of his religious profession.

3. Of the Blessed in heaven it is said, that "they
are come out of great tribulation." Religious, too,
may be truly said to have come out of many tribulations and afflictions. What is the world out of which
religious are delivered? Is it not full of mischief

and misery? full of sin, the greatest of all miseries?
full of ambition, criminal liberty and dangers innumerable, — a land of no Order, but of darkness,
inconstancy and perpetual confusion! Are not its
laws and maxims extremely pernicious? its examples deadly? Is it not full of men and devils who
unite to induce us to sin? How difficult for a
Christian to live in such a wicked world without any
attachment to its goods? how difficult to dwell in
the midst of pestilence and to escape contagion?
How difficult to stay the unsettled motions of the
heart from all manner of defilement, where the allurements of vanity are so many? How difficult to
breathe the noxious and pestilential atmosphere of the
world, and not to catch spiritual infections? Who
touches pitch and is not defiled? Every one knows
that the damnation of numberless souls is attribut-
able to the occassions of sin so common in the world.

And now when religious, moved by the grace of
God tried to leave Egypt—the world—when they
endeavored to withdraw themselves from the cruel
slavery of the world—the devil and the flesh; when
they were about to enter upon the land of promise—
the religious state—with what fierceness did not the
cruel Pharaoh—the world—set upon them? What
furious stormes did not the devil raise against them?
What violent opposition was not made by their
relatives and friends? But great, very great

indeed was the mercy of God over them. The Lord who called them out of Egypt to offer a perpetual sacrifice to Him in the Desert, fought for them, as if the cause was not theirs but His own. By the unspeakable strength of His Spirit; by an inestimable gift of His grace, He drew them from the vain conversations of the world, in which they were sometimes without God, or which is more detestable, against God, not ignorant of Him, but contemning Him. Under the command and the protection of God, they passed, "with palms in their hands," dry-shod through the Red Sea—the difficulties of the world,—they vanquished Pharaoh the devil, they overturned his chariots—carnal and secular desires—they took possession of the land of promise —the religious state; there, in the retirement of the cloister—they are far removed from their fierce enemies, and sing a joyful song in thanksgiving to Him, "Who cast the horse and rider into the sea."

St. Mary Magdalen de Pazzi had then good reason to embrace the walls of her convent, saying, "O blessed walls! O blessed walls! from how many dangers do you preserve me!" And blessed Mary Magdalen Orsini was right to say to those of her sisters in religion whom she saw laughing: "Laugh and rejoice, dear sister, for you have reason to be happy, being far removed away from the dangers of the world."

4. Again, of the Blessed in heaven it is said: "And He Who sitteth upon the throne, shall dwell over them." Of religious also the same may be said. They live in the house of God; they are His chosen people; they are always mindful of His divine Omnipotence and Goodness; in all their trials they say constantly to the Lord: "As the eyes of servants are on the hands of their masters— so are our eyes unto the Lord our God until He have mercy on us." Psal. 122, 2. For this reason when called upon by His servants, the Lord presently assists them; He sustains and protects them; He says to them: "Fear not, I am thy protector and thy reward exceedingly great." (Gen. 15.) You shall be My people, and I will be your God; I will give you one heart and one way, that you may fear Me all days, and that it may be well with you; I will close your wounds, and give you health; I will reveal to you the prayer of peace and truth; I will cleanse you from all your iniquities, whereby you have sinned against Me, and despised Me; you shall be to Me a name, and a joy, and a praise, and a gladness before all the nations of the earth, that shall hear of all the good things which I will do to you. Thus saith the Lord: There shall be heard in this place the voice of joy and the voice of gladness; the voice of the bridegroom and the voice of the bride; the voice of those that shall say: Give

glory to the Lord of hosts, for the Lord is good, and His mercy endureth forever; and the voice of those that shall bring their vows into the house of the Lord; I will make an everlasting covenant with you, and *I will not cease to do good to you.* I will plant you in this land in truth, with My whole heart and with all My soul; I will bring upon you all the good that I now speak to you. (Jerem. 32 and 33.) "He that toucheth you, toucheth the apple of My eye." (Zacharias II, 8.)

One day Jordanus, a man of great sanctity and the first general of the Black Friars after St. Dominic, clothed a novice in the holy habit of religion. Many of the young man's companions assisted at the ceremonies; they wept bitterly during the discourse which the blessed Jordanus made on the occasion. He told them that they should rather envy their friend, who had chosen the better part because religious serve God in the quality of gentlemen of the privy chamber to a Prince, with whom he is ever present and very familiar; whilst secular people, if they serve at all, serve as it were in the kitchen, or in some other inferior office. Reflect, then, seriously on the matter, and consider that the door is open for you also, if you wish to enter, and sit at table with the King of Kings. These words made a deep impression upon them. One of the company entered immediately, and all the rest followed his example soon after.

5. The Blessed in heaven "are in the sight of the Lamb." Religious too are always in the sight of the Lamb. The Son of God dwells among them in the Blessed Sacrament. They dwell with Him day and night under the same roof. They often visit Him,—they medidate constantly upon the life and passion of Jesus Christ; they imitate His example; they conform themselves to His holy will; they know that they are indebted to Him for the grace of their vocation and every good gift; on this account they cry with a loud voice: "Salvation to our God Who sitteth upon the throne, and to the Lamb, benediction and glory and wisdom and thanksgiving, honor and power for ever and ever." (Apoc. VII.) "They are in the sight of the Lamb," that is, they walk in the presence of God. For this reason, they are constantly on their guard not to offend the Lamb Who dwells with them. Those who live in the world defile their souls with daily stains, which they do not even perceive; for this is the property of a bad habit of sinning, that the more a man sins, the less he understands his sins, and the more he is delighted in sin. On the other hand, the more careful a man is of himself, the more he fears. However, "should a religious be unfortunate enough," says St. Alphonsus, "to fall into sin, he has the most efficacious helps to rise again. His rule which obliges him often to receive

the sacrament of penance, his meditations, and spiritual readings, in which he is reminded of the eternal truths, are powerful helps to rise from his fallen state.

"Again, should a religious go astray, his error will be instantly corrected ; the charitable admonitions of his superiors and companions in religion will soon make him repent of, and correct, his faults ; even the good example of his brothers will remind him continually of the transgression into which he has fallen. Surely, a Christian, who believes that eternal life is the one thing necessary, should set a higher value upon these helps to salvation than upon all the dignities and kingdoms of the earth.

'Moreover, as the world presents to seculars innumerable obstacles to virtue, so the cloister holds out to religious continual preventives of sin. In religion the great care which is taken to prevent light faults is a strong bulwark against the commission of grievous transgressions. If a religious resists temptations to venial sin, he merits by that resistance additional strength to conquer temptations to mortal sin ; but if through frailty he sometimes yields to them, all is not lost—the evil is easily repaired. Even then the enemy does not get possession of his soul ; at most he only succeeds in taking some unimportant outpost, from which he may be easily driven ; while, by such defeats, the religious is taught the necessity of greater vigilance and of stronger defences against future attacks. He is convinced of his own weakness, and being humbled and rendered diffident of his own strength, he recurs more frequently and with more confidence to Jesus Christ in the Blessed Sacrament and His holy Mother. Thus from these falls the religious sustains no serious injury ; since, as soon as he is humbled before the Lord, God stretches forth His all-powerful arm to raise him up. "When he shall fall, he shall not be bruised, for the Lord putteth His hand under him." On the contrary such victories over his weakness contribute to inspire greater diffidence in himself, and greater confidence in God. Blessed Egidius, of the Order of St. Francis, used to say, that one degree of grace in religion is better than ten in the world; because in religion it is easy to profit by grace, and hard to lose it; while in the world grace fructifies with difficulty, and is lost with ease."

6. Furthermore, of the Blessed in heaven it is said : "And the Lamb shall rule them, and lead them to the fountains of the waters of life." The same is true of religious The Lamb of God in the Blessed Sacrament enlightens, inflames and strengthens them with the waters of His grace. For the Lamb of God is among religious like a father of a family, as He was among the Apostles when

living on earth. What else are religious communities but so many colleges of the Apostles and societies of Jesus. "A religious," says St. Alphonsus, "is bedewed more frequently. O God, with what internal illuminations, spiritual delights, and sweetness of love does Jesus refresh the good religious at prayer, communion, in presence of the holy sacrament, and in the cell before the crucifix! Christians in the world are like plants in a barren land, on which but little of the dew of heaven falls, and from that little the soil for want of proper cultivation seldom derives fertility. Poor seculars! they desire to devote more time to prayer, to receive the Holy Eucharist, and to hear the word of God more frequently; they long for greater solitude, for more recollection, and a more intimate union of their souls with God. But temporal affairs, human ties, visits of friends, and restraints of the world, place these means of sanctification almost beyond their reach. But religious are like trees planted in a fruitful soil, which is continually and abundantly watered with the dews of heaven. In the cloister the Lord continually comforts and animates his faithful servants by infusing interior lights and consolations during the time of meditation, sermons, and spiritual reading, even by means of the good example of their companions. Well, then, might Mother Catherine of Jesus, of the holy Order of St.

4*

Teresa, say, when reminded of the labors she had endured in the foundation of a convent, "God has rewarded me abundantly by permitting me to spend one hour in religion in the house of His holy Mother."

7.   "They serve the Lord day and night."   In heaven, to praise God is the constant occupation of the saints, and in religion, every action of the community is referred to the glory of His name. "You praise God," says St. Augustine, "by the discharge of every duty ; you praise Him when you eat or drink ; you praise him when you rest or sleep." Religious praise the Lord by regulating the affairs of the community, by assisting in the sacristy, or at the gate ; they praise the Lord when they go to table ; they praise Him when they retire to rest and sleep ; they praise Him in every action of their life."

8.   *"They shall no more hunger or thirst."*   In heaven, the blessed have nothing more to desire. They enjoy perfect peace and happiness.   In religion, by means of the holy vows, all the poisoned sources of sin and irregular desires are cut off.   By the vow of chastity, all the pleasures of sense are forever abandoned ; by the vow of poverty, the desire of riches is perfectly eradicated ; and by the vow of obedience, the ambition of empty honors is utterly extinguished.   "Worldly goods;" St. Al-

phonsus says, "can never satisfy the cravings of the human soul." The brute creation, being destined only for this world, are content with the goods of the earth; but being made for God, man can never enjoy happiness except in the possession of the divinity. The experience of ages proves this truth; for if the goods of this life could content the heart of man, kings and princes who abound in riches, honors, and earthly pleasures, should spend their days in the enjoyment of perfect bliss and happiness. But history and experience attest that they are the most unhappy and discontented of men, and that riches and dignities are always the fertile sources of fears, of troubles, and of bitterness. The Emperor Theodosius entered one day, unknown, into the cell of a solitary monk, and after some conversation, said, "Father, do you know who I am? I am the Emperor Theodosius." He then added, "Oh! how happy are you, who lead here on earth a life of contentment, free from the cares and woes of the world. I am a sovereign of the earth, but be assured, Father, that I never dine in peace."

But how can the world, a place of treachery, of jealousies, of fears, and commotions give peace to men? In the world, indeed, there are certain wretched pleasures which perplex rather than content the soul; which delight the senses for a moment, but leave lasting anguish and remorse be-

4

hind. Hence the more exalted and honorable the rank and station a man holds in the world, the greater is his uneasiness, and the more racking his discontent. We may, then, conclude that the world, in which the heart-rending passions of ambition, advance, and the love of pleasures, exercise a cruel tyranny over the human heart, must be a place not of ease and happiness, but of inquietude and torture. Its goods can never be possessed to the full extent of our wishes; and when enjoyed, instead of infusing content and peace into the soul, they drench her with the bitterness of gall. Hence, whosoever is satiated with earthly goods, is saturated with wormwood and poison.

Happy, then, the religious who loves God, and knows how to esteem the favor which He bestowed upon him in calling him from the world and placing him in religion; where, conquering by holy mortification his rebellious passion, and practising continued self-denial, he enjoys that peace which according to the Apostle, exceeds all the delights of sensual gratification—"The peace of God, which surpasseth all understanding." Find me, if you can, among those seculars on whom fortune has lavished her choicest gifts, or even among the first princes or kings of the earth, a soul more happy or content than a religious divested of every wordly affection, and intent only on pleasing God. He is not rendered unhappy by poverty, for he preferred it before all the riches of the earth; he has voluntarily chosen it, and rejoices in its privations; nor by the mortification of the senses, for he entered religion to die to the world and himself; nor by the restraints of obedience, for he knows that the renunciation of self-will is the most acceptable sacrifice he could offer to God. He is not afflicted at his humiliations, because it was to be despised that he came into the house of God. "I have chosen to be an abject in the house of my God, rather than dwell in the tabernacles of sinners." Retirement is to him rather a source of consolation than of sorrow; because it frees him from the cares and dangers of the world To serve the community, to be treated with contempt, or to be afflicted with infirmities, does not trouble the tranquillity of his soul, because he knows that all these make him more dear to Jesus Christ. Finally, the observance of his rule does not interrupt the joys of a religious, because the labors and burdens which it imposes, however numerous and heavy they may be, are but the wings of a dove, which are necessary to fly to, and be united with, his God. Oh! how happy and delightful is the state of a religious whose heart is not divided, and who can say with St. Francis "My God and my all."

Let us be persuaded that neither pleasures of

sense, nor honors, nor riches, nor the world with all its goods, can make us happy. God alone can content the heart of man. Whoever finds Him possesses all things. Hence St. Scholastica said, "that if men knew the peace which religious enjoy in retirement, the entire world would become one great convent;" and St. Mary Magdalen de Pazzi used to say, "that they would abandon the delights of the world, and force their way into religion." St. Laurence Justinian says, that "God has designedly concealed the happiness of the religious state; because if it were known, all would relinquish the world and fly to religion."

The very solitude, silence, and tranquillity of the cloister, give to a soul that loves God a foretaste of Paradise. Father Charles of Lorena, a Jesuit of royal extraction, used to say that the peace which he enjoyed during a single moment in his cell was an abundant remuneration for the sacrifice he had made in quitting the world. Such was the happiness which he occasionally experienced in his cell, that he would sometimes exult and dance with joy. Arnolf, a Cistercian, comparing the riches and honors of the court which he had left with the consolations which he found in religion, exclaimed: "How faithfully fulfilled, O Jesus, is the promise which Thou hast made of rendering a hundred-fold to him who leaves all things for Thy sake!" We read of the monks of St. Bernard, who led lives of great penance and austerities, that they received, in their solitude, such spiritual delights, that they were afraid they should obtain in this life the reward of their labors.

9. Finally, "And God shall wipe away all tears from their eyes." In heaven the Blessed shall have no more sorrows The Lord will dry up the tears they have shed in this life. This also the Lord will do for religious, even in this life by mixing their tears of compunction and heartfelt sorrow with a holy joy of conscience and a profound peace of heart and other divine consolations. But it is particularly in the hour of death that religious will experience this truth, and appreciate the grace of their vocation to the religious life. "Some are deterred," says St. Alphonsus, "from entering religion by the apprehension that their abandonment of the world might be afterwards to them a source of regret. But in making choice of a state of life, I would advise such persons to reflect not on the pleasures of this life, but on the hour of death; which will determine their happiness or misery for all eternity. And I would ask, if, in the world, surrounded by seculars, disturbed by the fondness of children, from whom they are about to be separated forever, perplexed with the care of their worldly affairs, and troubled by a thousand scruples of

4*

conscience, they can expect to die more contented than in the house of God, assisted by their holy companions, who continually speak of God, who pray for them, and console and encourage them in their passage to eternity? Imagine you see, on the one hand, a prince dying in a splendid palace, attended by a retinue of servants, surrounded by his wife, his children, and relations, and represent to yourself, on the other hand, a religious expiring in his monastery, in a poor cell, mortified, humbled, far from his relatives, stripped of property and self-will; and tell me, which of the two dies more contented? Ah! the enjoyment of riches, of honors, and pleasures in this life, does not afford any consolation at the hour of death, but rather begets grief and diffidence of salvation ; while poverty, humiliations, penitential austerities, and detachment from the world, render death sweet, and give to a Christian increased hopes of attaining that true felicity which shall never end.

Jesus Christ has promised that whosoever leaves his house and relatives for God's sake shall enjoy enternal life. "And every one that hath left house, or brethren, or sisters, or father, or mother, or lands, for My sake, shall receive a hundred-fold, and possess life everlasting." A certain religions of the Society of Jesus being observed to smile on his death bed, some of his brethren who were present began to apprehend that he was not aware of his danger, and asked him why he smiled; he answered, "Why should I not smile, since I am sure of Paradise? Has not the Lord Himself promised to give eternal life to those who leave the world for His sake? I have long since abandoned all things for the love of Him. He cannot violate His own promises. I smile, then, because I confidently expect eternal glory." The same sentiment was expressed long before by St. John Chrysostom, writing to a certain religious: "God," says the saint, "cannot tell a lie; but He has promised eternal life to those who leave the goods of this world. You have left all these things; why, then, should you doubt the fulfillment of His promise?"

St. Bernard says that "it is very easy to pass from the cell to heaven; because a person who dies in the cell scarcely ever descends into hell, since it seldom happens that a religious perseveres in his cell till death, unless he be predestined to eternal happiness." Hence St. Lawrence Justinian says that religion is the gate of Paradise, because living in religion, and partaking of its advantages, is a great mark of election to glory. No wonder, then, that Gerard, the Brother of St. Bernard, when dying in his monastery, began to sing with joy and gladness. God Himself says: "Blessed are the dead who die in the Lord." And surely religious, who by the holy vows, and especially by the vows of obedience, or total renunciation of self-will, die to the world and to themselves, must be ranked amongst the number of those "who die in the Lord." Hence, Father Suarez, remembering at the hour of death, that all his actions in religion were performed through obedience, was filled with spiritual joy, and exclaimed that he could not imagine death could be so sweet and so full of consolation."

You will ask : Must a religious not be afraid of Purgatory ? St Alphonsus answers : "The defects committed, after profession, by a good religious, are expiated in this world by his daily exercises of piety, by his meditations, communions, and mortifications. But, if a religious should not make full atonement in this life for all his sins, his purgatory will not be of long duration. The many sacrifices which are offered for him after death, and the prayers of the community, will soon release him from suffering." If, for instance, a priest of the Redemptorist Society dies, every Father of the Province to which the deceased belongs has to say for him five masses, and the office of the dead. Supposing there are but one hundred Fathers in the Province, there will be said for him five hundred masses. Besides every lay-brother of the Society has to say for him the Rosary three times a day for a week, and all the good works performed by the members of that Province are offered up during a whole week for the repose of the soul of the deceased Father.

Moreover, in every house of the other Provinces of the Society a High Mass is celebrated and the office of the dead recited by all the Fathers and the rosary said by every lay-brother. Finally during the Octave of All-Saints, a solemn Requiem Mass is celebrated in every Church of the Society; the office for the dead is also recited by all the Fathers, and the rosary by all the lay-brothers, for the deceased members of the Society. Similar pious customs are found in all religious Orders and Congregations. Thus you see how true it is what St. Bernard says of a religious: "*Purgatur citius*"—his stay in purgatory will be short.

But if the consolations and joys of religious are so great in the hour of their death, what will they be in heaven? "A religious," says St. Bernard, "is more abundantly rewarded." "Worldlings," says St Alphonsus, "are blind to the things of God; they do not comprehend the happiness of eternal glory, in comparison of which the pleasures of this world are but wretchedness and misery. If they had just notions, and a lively sense of the glory of Paradise, they would assuredly abandon their possessions—even kings would abdicate their crowns— and, quitting the world, in which it is exceedingly difficult to attend to the one thing necessary, they would retire into the cloister to secure their eternal salvation."

Jesus Christ has promised, that "whosoever shall leave all things for His sake, shall receive a hundred-fold in this life, and eternal glory in the next." Can you doubt His words? Can you imagine that He will not be faithful to His promise? Is He not more liberal in rewarding virtue than in punishing vice? If they who give a cup of cold water in His name shall not be left without abundant remuneration, how great and incomprehensible must be the reward which a religious, who aspires to perfection, shall receive for the numberless works of piety which he performs every day!—for so many acts of morti-fication and of divine love which he daily refers to God's honor and glory! Do you not know that these good works which are performed through obedience, and in compliance with the religious vows, merit a far greater reward than the good works of seculars?

Although the religious state has lost much of its primitive splendor, we may still say, with truth, that the souls who are most dear to God, who have attained the greatest perfection, and who edify the church by the odor of their sanctity, are, for the most part, to be found in religion. How few are there in the world, even amongst the most fervent, who rise early in the morning to pray and sing the praises of God! How few who spend five or six hours each day in these or similar works of piety! Who practise fasting, abstinence, and mortification! How few who observe silence, or accustom themselves to do the will of others rather than their own! And, surely, all these are performed by the religious of every Order: even in convents where the discipline may be more or less relaxed, many are found, who aspire to perfection, observe the rules, and perform, in private, many works of supererogation. It is evident that the conduct of the generality of pious christians in the world cannot be compared with that of good religious. No wonder, then, that St. Cyprian called virgins, consecrated to God, the flower of the garden of the church, and the noblest portion of the flock of Jesus Christ. St. Gregory Nazianzen says, the religious "are the first fruits of the flock of the Lord, the pillars and crown of faith, and the pearls of the church." Jesus Christ once said to St. Teresa: "Wo to the world, but for religious." Ruffinus says, "It cannot be doubted, that the world is preserved from ruin by the merits of religious." "I hold as certain," says St. Alphonsus, "that the greater number of the seraphic thrones, which were left vacant by the fall of the unhappy associates of Lucifer, will be filled by religious." Out of the sixty, who during the last

3*

century were enrolled in the catalogue of saints, or honored with the appellation of blessed, all, with the exception of five or six, belonged to religious Orders. Brother Lacci, of the Society of Jesus, appeared after death to a certain person, and said that he and King Philip the Second were crowned with bliss, but that his own glory as far surpassed that of Philip, as the exalted dignity of an earthly sovereign is raised above the low station of an humble religious.

"The dignity of martyrdom," says St. Alphonsus, "is sublime; but the religious state appears to possess something still more excellent. The martyr suffers that he may not lose his soul; the religious suffers to render himself more acceptable to God. A martyr dies for the faith, a religious for perfection." "It is true," says St. Bernard, "the religious life is a martyrdom less frightful than that by which the body is tormented; but it is more painful on account of its duration." One day our Lord showed to St. Gertrude in a vision, the militant and the triumphant church mingling together; each took his place according to his merits. Those who lived holy lives in the married state were with the Patriarchs; those who merited to know the Divine Secrets were with the Prophets; those who labored for the instruction and edification of others were with the holy Apostles, and so on. But Gertrude observed that those who served God in the *religious state* were joined to the choirs of. martyrs; and as these were specially adorned in ·each member of their body in which they had suffered for their Lord, so the religious had some special reward for each act of self-restraint which they had performed, and they had the same merit as the martyrs, and received the same reward in heaven. For as they had no persecutors to shed their blood, they had offered themselves daily as a holocaust of sweetness to their God by their continued mortifications and restraints.

Certainly if we consider the particulars of all the great advantages of the religious state, we shall find, that in this one benefit of religion all that we can possibly desire is, in a manner, contained. Here we have perfect remission of all our former offences as in a second baptism; our flesh is tamed by sobriety; we are at leisure to think of heavenly things, and are separated from all that may in any way hurt our soul. The will of God is the rule of our actions, and all kind of virtue is in continual practice. Here we receive direction from Superiors; light from particular rules; abundance of inward grace: increase of merit; comfort in fraternal charity; mutual assistance, and part of all good works which are performed among us, and all of which are greatly ennobled and embellished by the golden link of our vows, and crowned at last at the hour of death with that security which a state so remote from the world, and bordering so near upon heaven and heavenly things, usually brings to us. To the accomplishment and perfection of all this concur the particular love, favor, and protection of God and our Blessed Lady,—a thing wonderfully to be esteemed both for the profit and pleasure which accompany it.

But the greater the merit of the religious life, and the more numerous are its advantages, the more ought we to consider by what means we may possess the field where so much treasure lies hidden; for we cannot have it for nothing, but must buy it, and buy it at the price that has been set on it by our Saviour; viz: selling all we have and buying it therewith. This is most exactly performed by entering religion, nor is it easy to say how it can be done otherwise. And we may here consider the goodness of God in not determining any sum of money or wealth, lest any person might be excluded from the purchase of a thing so precious; on the contrary, He has, in His Infinite Wisdom, ordained that the price, the sum and total of all felicity should be, not so much to give, as rather to forsake what we have, so that whether we have much or little, or nothing at all, we may be admitted to the purchase, if we only leave all, and retain nothing to ourselves. But in reality we only make an exchange for what is far better, purchasing so incomparable a treasure, at so easy a rate; a treasure in which we shall have the price we gave returned and infinitely mu'tiplied. With David praising the Lord for His wonderful gifts and exhorting the people of Israel to do the same, I say: Behold, now bless ye the Lord, all ye servants of the Lord: Who stand in the house of the Lord, in the courts of the house of our God. In the nights lift up your hands to the holy places and bless ye the Lord." Ps. 133. "Praise ye the Lord, for the Lord is good; sing ye to His name, for it is sweet. For the Lord has chosen Jacob unto himself; Israel for his own possession. Praise ye the Lord, Who alone does great wonders, Who brought Israel out of Egypt, with a mighty hand, and stretched-out arm. Who divided the Red Sea into parts, and brought out Israel through the midst thereof, and overthrew Pharaoh and all his host in the Red Sea."—"Bless the Lord, O my soul, and never forget all He hath done for thee. Blessed be the name of the Lord," because He has proved a Father, and Redeemer and Sanctifier to thee.

CHAPTER V.

ANSWERS TO OBJECTIONS.

ONE day God commanded Moses, the leader of His people in the desert, to send twelve spies, to reconnoitre the land of promise, which was at no great distance. The messengers on their return gave a most flattering account of the beauty and and fertility of the land which they had seen, and as a proof produced a huge bunch of grapes and other rich fruits thereof, but at the same time, ten of them gave so frightful an account of its inhabitants and fortified towns, that the hearts of the people were struck with mortal fear. Those hopes of the promised land, which had hitherto sustained them, seemed to be no more, and the power of God, which had so miraculously preserved them, was entirely forgotten. They revolted against their leaders, and began to deliberate upon the choice which they should make of some other chief to lead them back to Egypt. In the meantime, Joshua and Caleb, two of the twelve spies, did all in their power to quiet the people, and to convince them of the un-reasonableness of their fears; they assured them that, under the protection of God, who had shown Himself always ready to support them, they had nothing to apprehend, and that no enemy, however formidable in appearance, would be able to stand against them.

These men who by their misrepresentations of the land of promise, discouraged the people of God from attempting the conquest of it, were a figure of those who, by misrepresenting or decrying the religious state, discourage many souls from seeking in earnest and acquiring so great a good, and hereby securing to themselves a happy eternity. "There are many," says St. Paul, "of whom I have often told you, (and now tell you with tears in my eyes) that they are enemies of the Cross of Christ." (Philip. 3, 18.)

I will now proceed to refute the objections usually brought by these enemies of the Cross against the religious State. For your greater entertainment, my dear reader, I will lay before you these objections together with their refutation in a dialogue between Stanislas and Paul, two brothers. Stanislas feels himself called to the religious life and is about to embrace it. Paul, his elder brother, noticing in Stanislas this inclination and determination, tries to dissuade him from carrying out his intention. Listen to what both have to say on the subject.

Paul.—Stanislas, is it not great madness on your part to embrace the religious life ? What can betray greater folly than to renounce the world, its goods, its comforts, its pleasures, and its honors for a life of obscurity and privation ?

Stanislas.—Indeed, my heart feels overjoyed at the thought that I am not made for the world, but for God alone. How could I take any pleasure in the world, which is so full of deceit. It makes many fair promises and performs nothing, and when it appears to perform, it comes far short of what it promised. As to the pleasures of the world, they seem sweet when beheld at a distance ; but indulge in them and at once you will taste their bitterness. All the goods and pleasures of this world are like a fisher's hook. The fish is glad while it swallows the bait and spies not the hook ; but no sooner has the fisherman drawn up his line, than it is tormented within, and soon after comes to destruction from the very bait, in which it so much rejoiced. So it is with all those who esteem themselves happy in their temporal possessions. In their comforts and honors, they have swallowed a hook. But a time will come when they shall experience the greatness of the torment which they have swallowed in their greediness. What means then must be adopted to avoid these hooks?—We must shun the bait. If we are greedy of the bait, we cannot avoid the hook which is hidden under it, that is, eternal death and perdition. Whatever is not God, or does not directly tend to Him, serves as a bait to catch us. God alone and those things that lead to God, are the only good things, which cannot be evil, nor used by the devil for our destruction. All other things may be wrested by the enemy to our overthrow and it is in them that he lays his snares. Our only safe course, then, is to shun them all

The things of this world are of such a nature that if a man once meddle with them, he can hardly shake them off again. The love for earthly things is like bird-lime to our spiritual wings. If we covet them, we cleave to them

As love for these things necessarily follows the use of them, many sins are committed on account of them; such as robberies, usury, deceitful bargains, dissembling, flattery, slanders, and many other mean acts. While eager in the pursuit, or quiet in the joyful possession of wealth and honor, the course of our mind towards God, is retarded, and either we run not at all or so heavily and slowly that it is folly to say we run at all. Our soul can never be without some delight; it will please itself either in base and unworthy things, or in things high and noble; the more earnest it is in the pursuit of high delights, the more it loathes the inferior; and the more ardent its desire of the inferior, the

4

more coldly does it regard the higher. These two loves cannot dwell in one heart; the seed of supernatural charity cannot grow, where it is choked by the thorns of base delights. As soon as the mind spends itself upon outward things, it wanders, as it were, out of itself; and the farther it wanders from itself, the farther also it goes from God, because the kingdom of God is within us.

From all this we may easily understand the danger to which people are exposed in the world, and see plainly the happiness of a religious, who renounces all things; for this general renunciation of all earthly goods, not only invites, but even compels us to seek heavenly things. No doubt this is the chief reason why Jesus Christ advises us to forsake our kindred and sell all and give it to the poor; for knowing that the devil uses these as instruments to draw us to earthly things, our Redeemer bids us leave them all, that we may be forced, as it were, to seek heavenly things and keep our hearts fixed upon God. "Earth seems to me vile and contemptible when I contemplate heaven," said the great St. Augustine. St. Bernard having reached man's estate, was not slow to perceive that it is very hard to save one's soul in the world, and resolved to leave it. His parents and relatives loved him so much that, though full of faith and piety, they did their utmost to keep him amongst them. But Bernard

made them understand so well the happiness and
the advantages of the religious life, that he not only
obtained their consent to his project of embracing
it, but even prevailed on four of his brothers to follow him. It was only the youngest who remained
in the paternal house. At the end of six months,
these five young men quitted Chatillon-sur-Seine,
and passed by Fontaine, near Dijon, to ask their
father's blessing. They then set out for the Abbey
of Citeaux, where they were to pronounce their
vows. Crossing the court-yard of the Castle of
Fontaine, they perceived little Nivard, their younger
brother, playing with some children of his own age.
"Adieu, little brother Nivard," said they, "we are
going away; we leave you to inherit all our Father's
possessions; you shall have all our lands and all our
wealth." "Yes, yes," answered the wise child,
"you take heaven and leave me earth; the shares
are not equal, and I will not be satisfied with mine."
In fact, when little Nivard grew up, and his father
had no need of his services, he went to rejoin his
brothers in their monastery, and, in his turn, left
earth for heaven. (Ratisbonne, Life of St. Bernard.)

Truly, what greater madness than to resolve to
perish with that which perishes! What greater
wisdom than, in time, to forsake that which sooner
or later we must forsake! especially when we know
that if we forsake it voluntarily, we shall have in-

estimable rewards, whereas if we wait until it be taken from us, we may well look often for punishments, but certainly shall have we rewards.

Paul.—But if you have plausible reasons for renouncing the world, what reasons can you have for renouncing your liberty, dearer than which there is nothing in this world—a liberty of which a certain poet has said, that all the gold in the world will not pay for it? What madness to make yourself the slave of another and put your feet in fetters!

Stanislas.—Indeed, it would never occur to me to sell my liberty for all the gold and treasures of this world. But I am ready to give it up for the everlasting goods of heaven and for the sake of God. The religious life is a life of obedience; it is the yoke of Jesus Christ. Though a yoke, yet it is sweet; though a burden, it is light. Without a yoke, without a burden no man can come to joy everlasting; "for the way is narrow which leadeth to it," and it behoved Jesus Christ, the King of glory, to suffer and *so to enter into His glory.* The world has also its yoke and not only one, but many rough and heavy ones. The yoke of Jesus Christ, or the service of God is true freedom, and full of delights and comforts. By taking upon myself the sweet yoke of Christ, I shall receive a *crown,* for ashes; the oil of joy, for mourning; the cloak of praise, for the spirit of sorrow; and my heart shall rejoice, and my joy no man shall take from me. Let me explain. What can be more noble for a soul than to seek her own good? for one thing is good for one, another for another. *Now what is the good of each being?* It is that which makes the being better and more perfect. It is clear that inferior beings cannot make superior ones better and more perfect. Now the soul being immortal, is superior to all earthly, or perishable things. These, then, cannot make the soul better and more perfect, but rather worse than she is; for he who seeks what is worse than himself, makes himself worse than he was before. Therefore, the good of the soul can be only that which is better and more excellent than the soul herself is. Now God alone is this good—He being Goodness Itself. He who possesses God, may be said to possess the goodness of all other things; for whatever goodness they possess, they have from God. In the sun, for instance, you admire the light; in a flower beauty; in bread, the savor; in the earth, its fertility. All these have their being from God. No doubt, God has reserved to Himself far more than He has bestowed upon creatures. This truth admitted, it necessarily follows that he, who enjoys God, possesses in him all other things; and consequently, the very same delight which he would have taken in other things, had he enjoyed them separately, he enjoys in God,

-4*

in a for greater measure, and in a more elevated manner.   For this reason, St. Francis of Assisium often used to exclaim : "My God and my All"— a saying to which he was so accustomed, that he could scarcely think of anything · else, and often spent whole nights in meditating on this truth.

Certainly, true contentment is only that which is taken in the Creator, and not that which is taken in the creature ; a contentment which no man can take from the soul, and in comparison with which all other joy is sadness ; all pleasure, sorrow; all sweetness, bitter ; all beauty, foul ; all delight, affliction. It is most certain that "when face to face we shall see God, as He. is," we shall have most perfect joy and happiness.   It follows, then, most clearly, that, the nearer we approach to God in this life, the more contentment of mind and the greater happiness of soul, we shall enjoy ; and this contentment and joy is of the self-same nature as that which we shall have in heaven : the only difference is, that here our joy and happiness is small, whilst there it will be infinitely great.   He, then, is a truly wise man, who, here below, seeks God and endeavors to be united as much as possible with His Supreme Good.

But now let me ask, what course of life is better calculated than the religious state to find God and bring about the union of the soul with her Supreme Good ?   It is precisely this manner of life which aims at nothing else than the service of God, or the exact fulfillmentof the divine will.

What can be more reasonable than always to follow this course of life ; nay, even to bind our-selves by vows evermore to follow it? Happy fet-ters, blessed chains, these vows ! They are not the chains of a slave and the marks of captivity, as the children of the world falsely imagine, from whom the mysteries of the kingdom of heaven are hidden ; on the contrary, they are bright ornaments of *those who are truly free*—the children of God, to whom it is given to understand the mysteries of the king-dom of heaven.

Certainly, he is free who does what he himself wills. A just man, though he obeys the law, does nevertheless what he wills, because he desires the good which is commanded, and does it, not induced by force of the outward command, but of his own desire and inclination.

When a man directs a traveller in his way, no one can say that he forces him to go that way, be-cause the traveller desires it far more, than he who directs him ; so whatever is suggested to a religious in his spiritual way and journey, either by word or writing, he takes it, as behooves him, for his own good and salvation, of which he is very desirous. The good which he thus does, he does willingly and cheerfully, receiving and performing the commands

of his Superior, or of his rules, as if he did it naturally. So that there cannot be truer liberty than
that which religious enjoy ; for all their obligations
are the result of their own election and free choice.

But let me make this truth still plainer. No
rational creatures enjoy a better and greater liberty
than do the Saints in heaven ; for they cannot sin
any more. True liberty does not consist in being
able to commit sin. To be able to commit sin is no
power at all ; it is a mark of weakness and misery,
not of perfection. God Who is Supreme Liberty
and Who can do all things, cannot sin. To have
the power of sinning implies the possibility of becoming a slave of sin. Now the more this power of
sinning in man is lessened, the more this possibility
of slavery is lessened. Therefore the more free he
becomes ; and if this power of sinning in man is
entirely taken away, his liberty is perfect. Such
is the case of the Saints in heaven.

Now this power of sinning is lessened by taking
the vows of religion, especially that of obedience,
for by these vows we bind our will always to do the
will of God. O happy necessity, which continually
urges man to do what is best. It is, therefore, a
great advantage for a man's free will to be thus
bound ; for by this means it is not destroyed, but
rendered more perfect, conformed as it is, to the
rule of all perfection—the will of God. I have then

good reason to rejoice in thus binding myself by vows. It is by them that I renounce that kind of liberty, which I could not make use of without great danger to myself. Were I to walk towards a precipice, my friends would do me a great favor by barring my passage in such a manner as to make it impossible for me to advance regardless of my own wishes. Now if I wish to run into the gulf of hell, I have but to follow the way of my own will. "If there were no self-will," says St. Bernard, "there would be no hell." Consequently to bar to me the passage that leads to destruction is to do me the gratest good.

Hence, the vows of religion in no way deprive a man of liberty. On the contrary, he who binds himself by them enjoys a more perfect liberty; for true liberty consists in being master of one self, and he who is thus bound and united to God is, without doubt, more his own master than he who is not thus bound. To illustrate :

Ask a man whose heart is set on earthly gain, what he thinks of those who renounce all to follow Christ and purchase heaven ; ask him, I say, whether they do wisely ? Certainly, he will answer, they do wisely. Ask him again, why he himself does not do what he commends in others ? He will answer : It is because I cannot. Why can you not ? Because avarice will not let me. It is because he is not free ; he is not master of himself nor of what he possesses. If he is truly master of himself and of what he has, let him lay it out to his own advantage ; let him exchange earthly for heavenly goods ; if he cannot, let him confess, that he is not his own master, but a slave to his love of money.

Again my inducement to make the vow of chastity is my hope, by the grace of God, to become so far master of myself as to keep this virtue. And what prevents another from taking this vow is, the fact that he does not believe that he is sufficiently master of himself to be able to keep it. Thus you see that of the two, I have the greatest power over myself to do what I wish; and to do what I believe I ought to do. But it is precisely in this that liberty consists. For the liberty which another keeps for himself, is not a true liberty ; it is a subjection, nay, even a slavery ; because, in reality, like a slave, he obeys his passion which has the mastery over him, and which drags him into sin. He is a slave to his passion "which leads him captive to the law of sin." (Rom. VII, 23.) For he who is overcome is a slave to him who overcame him ; wherefore, "whosoever sins is a slave to sin." (John VIII, 34.)

It is the same in regard to obedience. What moves me to make the vow of obedience is the confident hope by the assistance of God, to have so much power over myself as always to follow the will of my Superior. And that which prevents another from taking the same vow, is his conviction that he has not so much power over himself as to be able to renounce his own will, and to submit to that of another. You see then clearly, that I have more power over myself and more real liberty by subjecting myself to the yoke of obedience, than has the other person who is not able to do so. As therefore all those are slaves, who can only do as vice suggests, so, on the other hand, all those are truly free, who live according to virtue. Thus there is a real greatness and dignity in carrying the yoke of obedience; it is indeed this kind of yoke to carry which the Holy Ghost exhorts us in these words: "Put thy feet into her fetters, and thy neck into her chains; bow down thy shoulder, and bear her, and be not grieved with her bands." (Eccles. VI, 25.) Thrice happy chains, that give liberty to those who bear them!

It is, then, quite certain, that the greatness of our liberty is in proportion to the power which our will has to *will* and to *do* what God wishes us to do. But let it be remembered, that the greater this power is, the greater is also the goodness and perfection of our will; and the greater the perfection of our will, the greater is also the perfection of all its good actions; for the goodness and merit of our actions, is in proportion to the goodness of our will. To illustrate:—A man who is hardened in sin offends God more grievously when he sins, than another who sins out of frailty or from a sudden outburst of passion, because he sins by a will determined to evil, which is to sin against the Holy Ghost; so, in like manner, all those good actions which proceed from a will quite determined to what is good, are, doubtless, of far greater perfection and merit, than any others can be. The greater the artist, the more valuable is his work. So before God, the better the will, the better and more meritorious are all its good actions.

Another illustration of what has been said: Every action of Jesus Christ is of an infinite merit, because in Him the Divinity is so united to the Humanity as to make but one person. If we substitute, for our will, the will of God as the rule and basis of our actions, every one of them will be, as it were, of an infinite value, being, as they are, actions of the Divine will rather than of our own. Now, it is precisely by obedience that we substitute the Divine will for our own; and thus acquire infallibly that constancy determination of the will to adhere to what is good, which constancy is looked upon by theologians as one of the chief conditions of virtue.

By obedience we acquire this goodness or perfec-

tion of the will much faster than by any other
means. Let a soul practise, for a certain length of
time, all virtues without practising that of obedience,
and let another soul, during the same length of
time, practise perfect obedience, and rest assured,
that the latter will surpass the former in merits, in
grace, in union with God, and in heavenly glory
hereafter, far more than the light of the sun sur-
passes that of the dimmest star. A soul earnestly
endeavoring to practise perfect obedience, will, by
degrees, become so united with God as not to be
able to will except what God wills; but not to be
able to will except what God wills, is, as it were,
to be what God is, with whom to *will* and to *be* is
but one and the same thing; for to whomsoever
power is given to become a child of God, to him is
also given power not, indeed, to be God Himself, but
to be what God is.

To a soul thus disposed, the Lord grants such
great favors as it is impossible to describe. He
gives her a faith so lively, a confidence so firm, a
charity so ardent, a zeal for the salvation of her
neighbor so burning, a degree of prayer so sublime;
a prudence so unusual, a courage in all difficulties
so invincible, a peace so profound, a humility and
simplicity of heart so admirable, and sometimes
even a spirit so prophetic, together with a gift of
performing miracles so extraordinary as to make

every one exclaim : "Truly, that soul can say with St. Paul : 'I live, now not I, but Christ liveth in me.'" (Gal. ii., 20.)

Father Nieremberg relates that Father Louis de Guzman, when a novice, was very much tempted to leave the Novitiate and return to the world. Now, it happened one day that he saw a little bird which had escaped the cage and seemed to enjoy its liberty very much. But, all on a sudden, there came a hawk and carried it off and devoured it. At this moment Father Louis felt an inspiration of God which told him that, were he to return to the world and enjoy his liberty, he would fall into the snares of the devil, and thus lose not only the true liberty of the children of God, but even the kingdom of heaven itself.

Paul.—But is there not more than one road to heaven ? Can you not find God and serve Him in every place ? Can you not observe the command-ments of God and do His holy will in every state of life just as well as in the religious state ? Why do you wish to take the most difficult road ?

Stanislas.—You say that I can serve God every-where ; why then should I not select the best of all places, the house of the Lord itself ? Would you not prefer to serve a king in his palace as a great lord rather than on his farm as a common servant ? According to your opinion, one who is a slave of the

Turks, might serve God just as well and be satisfied; and yet all who have the misfortune to fall
into their slavery, try to obtain means for their de-
livery, in order to serve God and keep His commandments in a far better country.

Paul.—Be that as it may; you cannot deny
that one may be saved in every state of life?

Stanislas.—I cannot agree with you in that. I
know there is no express command to embrace the
religious life; every one is left free to do so or not.
But if a man has to undertake a long voyage, and
if the admiral of the fleet should invite him into
his own new and strongly built vessel, well provided with all necessaries, do you think he would
refuse his courtesy and throw himself into a weather-
beaten vessel, whose sea worthiness has been declared
doubtful? Would he not rather, with many thanks,
accept the offer? or even perhaps entreat to be admitted? Much more, therefore, to avoid the shipwreck of the soul, which is a loss eternal, ought I to
choose that state which may carry me safe through
the dangerous rocks and seas of this world. St.
Gregory says, that some cannot otherwise be saved.
Not every state of life suits every person. The
shortest and safest road to heaven is undoubtedly
the best. The religious state is that road, and he
who chooses it must certainly be believed to have
chosen the better part.

Paul.—You are too much afraid of the world; you represent it to yourself worse than it is in reality. I know many living in the world who most exactly comply with all the duties of their state; who give to Cæsar what belongs to Cæsar, and to God what belongs to God. No one could live more safely in the world than you; for you are filled with the fear of the Lord; you are possessed of great talents and a truly practical judgment.

Stanislas.—You know, that St. John the Apostle fitly divides the whole kingdom of this world into three parts; he says that "all that is in this world, is the concupiscence of the flesh, the concupiscence of the eyes, and the pride of life." How foul and abominable a body must that be, which is composed of three so foul and abominable members! I cannot be deceived in believing what this great Apostle teaches of the world, nor can I be wrong in withdrawing from such a pestiferous place.

Paul.—No, I cannot agree with you. According to your opinion, all would have to leave the world for the convent, and if all should become religious, the world would perish.

Stanislas.—What do you think would become of the world if there were no mechanics and no farmers, but if all were kings, presidents, or princes? And yet you would prefer to be a Nobleman rather than a simple peasant. Religious constitute the nobility of heaven, and are the princes of the people of God. Every one, therefore, should, were he called, embrace the religious state, and thank God for the grace of calling him to be a nobleman and prince in His kingdom.

You say: If all should become religious, the world would perish. Would to God that all would become religious; heaven, the city of God, would much sooner be filled and the end of the world hastened. Were it not better that the *Kingdom of God were come*, which we daily beg, and that God were *all in all*. And if it should so happen that all should be chaste and lead a single life, it would be an evident sign of the will of God, that the world should soon end; and truly, it could not come to a better end!

But fear not lest all should be virgins. Virginity is a hard thing, and because it is hard, it is rare. There are many to whom God, out of His secret judgments, does not vouchsafe so great a benefit; others He calls to be partakers of it, and they give no ear to His calling, but charmed with the pleasures of this life, cannot free their feet from the nets in which they are entangled. And not only does the infirmity of man hinder this benefit from becoming ordinary, but it belongs also to the provident wisdom of the Almighty to have a care, that there be always some to attend to posterity, so long as it is

5*

His will that this world should last.   He manifests His Providence in watching over the very beasts and worms of the earth, preserving everything in kind as it was created.   So no man can fear that God will forsake mankind.

Paul.—I have often heard priests speak unfavorably of Religious Orders; many a priest opposes them as much as he can, saying that they put their scythe into other people's harvests, etc.   Why would you, then, embrace a state which is so much disliked by many otherwise excellent priests?

Stanislas.—Be not surprised at such murmurs and complaints.   We read in the Gospel that Martha murmured at Mary, who had chosen the better part.   The number of priests who oppose Religious Orders can be but very small.   They repent, in the end, of what they said or did against them.   Guillaume de Saint Amour published a libel against the Religious Orders of his time.   But at the end of his life, he is said to have confessed that he had been actuated by envy at the Mendicant Orders; and to prove that he repented from his heart, he left his body to be buried with the Friar Preachers.   In like manner, Laurentius Anglicus, after persecuting the Friars, when he came to die at Paris, left them all his books, and, wonderfully penitent, desired to be buried in their monastery.   The sentiments of all good priests for Religious Orders are expressed in the following remarkable words of Bourdoise, a celebrated parish-priest in the reign of Louis XIII.: "It is an injustice," he says, "when priests prevent the people from applying to monks. It does not edify them when they hear priests complain of monks, as if there were not enough work for both priests and monks. As for me, if I may be allowed to say what I think, in my conscience, I believe that without monks, that is, if there had not been monks, we should at present be without faith and without religion, or at least a hundred times worse than we are. I hope I may not give displeasure to priests, but God grant that they do not deceive themselves. If a priest have any portion of the spirit of the tonsure, if he does not want monks in his parish, he will at least take care to live in peace and good understanding with them."

Another secular priest, Peter of Blois, speaking of the monks in general, says: "The life of monks, of whom there are divers kinds,—for the tunic of Joseph is of many colors, and the spouse of Christ is clothed with variety—I venerate with all the affection of my heart, and I embrace their feet with the arms of most devout humility; for I know that above all seculars, whether clerics or laics, they adhere more closely to the footsteps of the Apostles; truly, in the bowels of Christ every holy Order I love, I magnify, I venerate and adore. For a long time I used to have always with me some man of a Religious Order, a witness of my conversation, and a guardian-angel of my body and soul; but above all, I loved one, dear to God and men, who from being rich made himself poor for Christ. In his friendship, I glory, preferring it to all my relations with the court in the palace. Doubtless he is the friend of God. Honey and milk are on his tongue, and his countenance is composed to a joyful serenity, with a certain expression of angelic peace. His memory I place as a seal upon my heart." (Peter Blois Cont. Depravatorem.)

Indeed, you will search in vain through all Christian history to find an example of a good priest or prelate who, besides evincing a personal affection and reverence for the Religious Orders, did not recognize and proclaim loudly, like the illustrious confessor of the Rhine, Clement Augustus de Droste-Vischering, Archbishop of Cologne, that monasteries are absolutely necessary to each diocese, for various important and indispensable ends of pastoral care, which can never be accomplished without them. The ancient bishops, like Fulgentius, even built monasteries in which they might live with monks when their other duties were fulfilled, so anxious were they to perfect themselves in that discipline which they were bound to maintain amongst the clergy.

frightful and obstinate murder committed by the parents of the child.

"Wo, three times wo, wo forever to those parents, who make division with their children, when they hear My voice! Happiness and benediction for ever to those parents and their children who hear and receive it."

In his exposition of the 4th and 25th Psalms, Father Alexander Faia, of the Society of Jesus, relates that at Tudela, in Old Castile, a very rich man had an only son, whom he had destined to perpetuate the family. But the son, being called to the Society of Jesus sought admission with so much earnestness that the Superiors at length received him. After the novitiate, the father came and made so many complaints that, to please him, the son returned to the world. But he felt himself again called to forsake the world. Being unwilling to return to the Society, he entered into the Order of St. Francis. But the father induced him the second time to renounce the religious state. Listen to what happened. The father wished the son to marry a certain person; the son preferred another for his wife. They began to contend and quarrel with each other; and one day in a dispute the son killed the father; he was convicted of the crime, and executed on a gibbet.

"O! how many families," exclaimed St. Alphonsus, "have been ruined on account of parents making children give up their vocation ! How many parents shall we see condemned in the valley of Josaphat, for having thus caused their children to lose their vocation! What greater source of consolation can parents have than to see a son or a daughter consecrated to God, and leading the life of a saint?"

Paul.—Stanislas, I think this instruction is well calculated to move father and mother to give you their consent and blessing; but should they not do so, would you feel justified in leaving them without their consent?

Stanislas.—Irregular affection towards parents or kindred is one of those powerful engines used by the devil to undermine religious vocations. St. Jerome fitly calls this affection the ram or warlike instrument to batter down piety and devotion. All those who feel themselves called to the religious life must arm themselves against this great temptation. Let us, then, be firmly convinced, and hold as an infallible maxim that when once assured of the will of God calling us to religion, whatever afterwards occurs to divert or draw us from our vocation, must be a devilish temptation. He tempts all, but much more so those of whom it is written : "His food is the elect." It is one of his greatest artifices to conquer by the importunities of those who are particularly dear to us.

To overcome this temptation, we must make the following reflection. Our love towards God must have no limits; it admits of an infinite increase; hence our charity should become every day more fervent towards Him Who commands us to love Him "with our whole heart, with our whole soul, and with all our strength," but the love of our neighbor has its limits; for we are commanded to love our neighbor as ourselves; and to outstep these limits, by loving him as much as we love God, were a crime of the blackest enormity. "If a man come to Me," says our Lord, "and hate not his father and mother, and wife and children, and brethren and sisters, yea and his own life also, he cannot be My disciple," and "he that loveth father or mother more than Me, is not worthy of Me." Parents, no doubt, are to be affectionately loved and highly respected; but religion requires that supreme honor and homage be given to Him alone who is the Sovereign Creator and universal Father, and that our love for our parents be referred to our eternal Father who is in heaven. Should, however, our parents be at any time opposed to the will of God in our regard, we are, of course, to prefer the will of God to the desires of our parents, always keeping in view the divine maxim: "we ought to obey God rather than men." It is better to sadden our parents than the sweet heart of Jesus; it is better to have them for our enemies than God.

It is, therefore, an undoubted principle of theology, that in this case we owe no obedience at all to our parents. Divines give solid reasons for this. St. Thomas Aquinas says, that as to the nature of the body, all men are equal among themselves; a servant is not inferior to his master, nor a child to his parent. Hence no man can reasonably be compelled either to marry or to live a single life for other men's or his own father's pleasure.

As to the commandment to honor our parents, we say with St. Augustine, that we must both honor our parents, and yet, without any want of piety, may disregard them, in order to preach the kingdom of heaven, because we honor them according to their rank and degree; but when that honor becomes an obstacle to the love of God, then we must neglect it and shake it off.

The power of parents over their children is a participation of the authority of God, *from whom all paternity* is derived; it is but the power of a deputy or delegate. Therefore, if God commands one thing and a parent another, no one can doubt that the power and jurisdiction of a parent ceases, because it is opposed to the will of Him who gave that power. God, then, is the cause, and the only cause, why it is lawful for us not to obey our parents, for "who loveth father and mother more than Me is not worthy of Me." "Though your mother,"

Stanislas.—No man of common sense and ex-perience will, for a moment, entertain the illusion, that abstemiousness and constant good order in all things have any tendency to shorten human life. Who are those that are almost continually troubled with indigestion, and restlessness and are oftener and more dangerously sick? Are they not those who live luxuriously and on dainties? Religious people, besides the spiritual blessings which they enjoy, have also better health of body, than those wo are delicately brought up, and commonly con-sidered happy. These are as if they were bred in a quagmire, tender and effeminate, and more subject to all kinds of diseases. I know some persons, and I have heard of many, far more delicate than my-self who embraced the religious life and became very strong and robust in it, and complied with all its obligations for more than fifty or sixty years. Regularity in every thing, which is nowhere greater than in religion, is, according to all experience, the best preservative of life. Every one knows that as grief and passion exhaust the spirits and are, as it were, a torture or drag upon the life of man, so the peace of mind of a religious, and the happiness of his soul must necessarily preserve health and pro-long life on account of the affinity between soul and body. Daniel and his companions abstained from the meat and wine of the King of Babylon, and

4

succeeded better with beans and water, than all the other children who ate of the King's meat. The numerous examples of longevity amongst religious who practised the most rigid austerities ought to be conclusive on this point.

Besides, every Religious Order takes particular care not only of the soul of each of its members, but also of the body. I know for certain that the best parents could not take more and better care of the health of their children than Religious Orders do of that of their subjects. Not long ago I happened to read the rule of a certain Religious Order on this subject, and to my great astonishment I learned, that the Superiors were bound to sell even the chalices of the church, if necessary, in order to defray the expenses for the preservation or recovery of the health of their subjects.

Paul.—I know several religious persons, who, in the discharge of their hard obligations, have undermined their health completely. God does not always work miracles.

Stanislas.—And do you not see and hear every day that far more persons in the pursuit of worldly affairs, and in the service of the world, ruin their health and come to an early grave? But to shorten and even to close our life in the service of God, is to save it. "Whosoever shall lose his life for My sake and for the Gospel, shall save it." (Mark. 8,

35.) If soldiers generously sacrifice their lives in the service of an earthly King, how much more generously ought not we to sacrifice our lives in the service of our heavenly King, Who first sacrificed His for our sake? It matters very little to live long, but it is an affair of the greatest importance to lead a holy life. A holy life is a long life before God, because He will crown it with eternal happiness. He who discovers a gold mine becomes richer in a day than another who worked hard for fifty years. The religious life is that hidden treasure, or gold mine, of which the Gospel speaks; or rather, religion contains an infinite treasure, because it has within it such abundance of wealth, not of one kind only, but all manner of wealth heaped in a mass together. Now, he who finds a treasure has, as I have just said, great advantage over one who is rich by trading or otherwise. For he who trades acquires his wealth by much pain and labor, runs many risks and is a long time collecting it; but he who finds a treasure lays hold on it at once, without labor or danger, and is in a moment raised to exeessive wealth. So secular people increase their stock of virtue, by much and long striving, and sometimes they suffer shipwreck, and in one hour lose all that they had laid up in many years, by falling into one mortal sin, a misfortune of frequent, yea, of daily occurrence, and no wonder, in a sea so full of shoals and tempests! One, however, who has entered into religion has found a great treasure. The state itself and vocation breathe, as it were, into his heart the spirit of poverty, and particular affection for chastity and obedience and other virtues as things contained in the very spirit of religion. To die after having lived in this state but a short time, is to leave this world with immense merits for eternal life. The wordly minded do not understand this; it is hidden from them. Did they but know what it is, they could hardly resist the desire of laying hold on this treasure of the religious life. To spend then but a short life in religion, is far better than to live ten times longer in the world.

Paul.—I know several young persons who entered into religion, with the best intentions and in good health, but were dismissed, after some time on account of ill health. Were the same to happen to you, you would become a burden to yourself and to others.

Stanislas.—I thought of this myself and felt a little afraid. So I went to see a holy priest, a Superior of a religious community, and consulted him on the subject. He gave me the following reply: "Novices," he said, "who are too easily discontented, who murmur, complain and fret at the least inconvenience, who are too much concerned about their health and too tender of themselves will never make good members in religion. This tenderness or superfluous love for their bodies makes them too attentive not only to the least ill which they may feel, but will also fill them constantly with apprehension as to those which might happen, causing them to lament and murmur that they are not well treated and assisted, that they want this or that. Such like reflections are far from generous minds. Hence, it is an infallible maxim, that persons tender for their bodies, are also of a pusillanimous mind. This proceeds from a want of generosity. Such persons generally fill the monastery with tears, complaints and lamentations; they are usually melancholy and fretful, very often discouraged, taking difficulties for impossibilities and believing everything that is disagreeable to be insupportable; and to maintain their cause, they form many sad and scandalous complaints against the rules, and those who govern. If they are reproved for their softness of disposition and their tiresome humor, they redouble their complaints, murmuring that there is no charity because others do not weep and lament with them, or pity them, and they protest that they have very great cause to be afflicted. Should they be sick, if others are not occupied with describing the immensity of their sufferings, and with running up and down to seek every remedy their fancy suggests, they look upon themselves, as

4*

of all others, the most miserable and neglected; then they think every one is devoid of pity. In fine, persons of this description are always on the watch to see if more be done for others than for themselves, self-love suggesting to their fancy that there is not so much done for them as is requisite. This softness both of body and mind is one of the greatest evils in the religious life; and superiors must be very careful not to receive those who are considerably attacked with it; because they do not wish to be cured refusing to make use of what could give them health. So you see, my young friend, that no Order could keep a sickly novice of this disposition.

Besides there are certain diseases which cannot be properly treated in a religious community, or which it is easy to foresee will ultimately affect the mind. No novice afflicted with them can reasonably require to be suffered to remain. Let such a novice not repine, if he is dismissed—he will not fail to receive his reward for his good desire and the efforts which he made to become a religious. If the Lord has chosen the religious state as a channel through which He bestows great graces, He has not, for that, deprived Himself of the means to bestow just as great graces upon souls of a good will, who are forced by circumstances to live in the world. Let them build for themselves a convent out of the will of God; let them stay in it in all patience, and the Holy Ghost will not fail to direct and assist them. But novices, the wise Superior continued, whose constitution is delicate, or whose health has been so impaired during the time of their probation, as to leave no hope of recovery, will be allowed to remain provided they be generous souls. Now generous souls do not easily complain; they earnestly try to be patient and resigned to the holy will of God; they tell their sufferings without exaggerating, leaving the care of applying the remedies to the one charged with it, and contenting themselves with suffering lovingly and keeping close to God. Such souls as these show that they are in earnest in applying to perfection; they give edification to every one, and draw down the blessing of God upon a whole community. Therefore, they are suffered to remain in the convent.

Hence it is that some holy founders of Religious Orders, admitted into their Orders such weak, delicate, and deformed persons, as were generous souls, gifted with a strong mind, a firm will and good heart. Such souls if afflicted with bodily infirmities, become great saints, true gems in a religious community, and a source of great blessings for the whole Order. Assuredly, no Superiors will have so little piety as to frustrate the great design of God in such souls by dismissing them from His House

where He called them that in them might come true
what is said in the Gospel : 'This sickness is not
unto death, but for the glory of God, that the Son
of God may be glorified by it.'" (John. 11, 4.)

This consoled me very much, and my fears van-
ished altogether when, a few days ago, I happened
to read the sentiments of St. Alphonsus on this subject.   This Saint was greatly afflicted at seeing a
good novice sick, and when the Fathers, at times,
wished to send him home, the Saint himself became
his advocate.   "There is," said he, "no law ex-
cluding from the house of God one who has left all
to follow Him. If the physicians employed, and
the remedies used in the Order, cannot restore his
health, it is not probable that it will improve under
the paternal roof, and if God wills that he should
soon die, it is better for him to die in religion than
in the midst of the world.   What mother was ever
so unnatural as to expel her child from the house
for being sick." It was the opinion of the Saint,
that those novices who were pious and patient in
illness, assisted the Order by their example ; for as
they were themselves pleasing to God, they drew
down His blessing on others, and when a fervent
novice was at the point of death, St. Alphonsus was
never distressed, but rejoiced in the assurance that
such a one was happy.   But when a sick novice
wished to leave the Order, he granted the permis-

sion only with pain. (Tannoja's Life of St. Alphonsus, II vol, chapt. 63.)

Now, my dear brother, should I become sick, I will try to be a generous soul—I will beseech the Lord earnestly to give me grace to comply with the designs which He has in thus afflicting me, in order that His own glory and my sanctification may result from it. "Because He hoped in Me," says the Lord, "I will deliver him, and I will protect him. He shall cry to Me, and I will hear him; I am with him in tribulation; I will deliver him, and I will glorify him; I will fill him with length of days, and I will show him My salvation." (Ps. 90.)

Paul.—Stanislas, did you ever tell father and mother about your intention ?

Stanislas.—I have not done so as yet for very good reasons.

Paul.—What good reason can a dutiful child have to conceal such a design from his parents? Does not this betray a great want of filial affection ? In this you certainly do not follow the example of pious children. I read, not long ago, how Wenceslaus, the son of Leo, a celebrated General of the Emperor Ferdinand III.. acquainted his parents, even in his childhood, of his intention of becoming a religious. I cannot account for your secrecy.

Stanislas.—I suppose you read at the same time, how the parents of Wenceslaus rejoiced at seeing

their son called to so holy a life ; how they thanked
God for this great grace how they did all in their
power to encourage him in his holy resolution, and
how they f____ed his entrance into religion, and
how when o_..._e-point of leaving for the Society of
Jesus, his mother told him that, should he leave
the Society, she would never look upon him again
as her son.

St. Louis of Gonzaga was the oldest child of the
family. However when his mother, the marchioness
of Castiglione, saw that her son was called to the
Society of Jesus, she endeavored to facilitate his
entrance into religion.

Great indeed are the blessings which God showers
down upon such pious parents.   He does not allow
Himself to be surpassed in generosity.   He rewards
them with the hundred-fold of spiritual and temporal
blessings for the sacrifice which they thus make of
one or more of their children.

Unfortunately, my parents and those of many
others do not happen to be so generous towards
God. When one of their children resolves to embrace the religious life, they become his worst ad-
versaries.   Instead of blessing the' child and con-
gratulating him on the choice of so holy a state of
life, they turn in anger against him ; either from
worldly interest or misplaced affection, they become
the enemies of their child's spiritual welfare.   The

words of our Lord come true in their regard. ' The enemies of a man are those of his own household." (Matt. 10, 36.) What is most strange is, that even such parents as generally pass for pious people scruple not in the least, under any pretexts whatever, to employ all their powers to prevent their children from following the call of God. We read in the life of F. Paul Segneri, the younger, that his mother, although a lady of great piety, left no means in her power untried to obstruct the vocation of her son, whom God called to religion. Also in the Life of the Right Rev. Dr. Cavalieri, Bishop of Troyes, we are told that his father, though a very pious man, tried every means to prevent his son from entering into the Congregation of the Pious Laborers, (as he afterwards did,) and even went so far as to enter a process against him in the ecclesiastical court. And how many other parents do we behold, who, from being devout persons of prayer, seem to be quite changed, and behave in such cases as if they were governed and possessed by the devil; for hell never seems to arm itself so strongly as when it is employed in hindering from the accomplishment of his vocation one whom God has called to the religious state. Under such circumstances it is in the opinion of the Fathers of the Church, more advisable to keep our vocation secret, for fear of losing it.

Paul.—How do you know that Father and Mother will oppose you?

Stanislas.—They have uttered their sentiments on this subject on several occasions. Not long ago, when our cousin Charles entered religion, they expressed most decidedly their antipathy to the religious life; they said they hoped that none of their children would ever conceive the idea of becoming a religious. I know that it is a sin for my parents to be so much opposed to the religious life. Their sin, however, may perhaps find some excuse in the fact, that they are not sufficiently instructed on this subject. But as, in a few days, our cousin John is to enter the Society of Jesus, the conversation will, of course, turn again on the subject of the religious life. I will then not fail to explain to my parents their duties on this point; I will tell them what I read, some time ago, in a book treating on the duties of parents, namely: Let parents remember, that God is the Supreme Master of their children; they are His gift; His claim to them is indisputable; as He has a right to call them out of this life at any moment He pleases, so He can also call them to His service. No father or mother can dispute this right without being a most execrable blasphemer. Now to prevent a child from following the call of God, is to dispute this supreme right of the Almighty, which, of course, is a great sin.

God gives to each man his vocation, and chooses for him a state in which He designs that he should serve Him. This is according to the order of predestination described by St. Paul, the Apostle, when he writes: "Whom He predestinated, them He also called; and whom He called, them He also justified and glorified." (Rom. 8, 30.) He then who desires to insure his salvation, must carefully follow the divine inspiration in the choice of that state of life to which God calls him; for it is in that state that God has prepared for him the aids which are requisite, in order to attain salvation; it is in that state only that he has well-grounded hopes to be saved. Now it is the duty of parents to assist and induce their children to become saints, by letting them follow that road by which God calls them. To prevent their children from following the voice of God, would be a very grievous sin for parents. As it is an act of great injustice in a man unlawfully to prevent another from taking hold of a great good to which he has a just title, so the act of injustice is still far greater in parents, when they unreasonably prevent their children from acquiring one of the greatest of all goods—the religious life.—For beyond all doubt, to impugn the counsel of God, to destroy that which He builds, to scatter abroad that which He gathers, to cut off the soldiers whom He musters under His standard, is nothing else than to join in

5

league with the devil, and wage war against God. This is an enormous offence, in which St. John Chrysostom finds nine degrees of malice. St. Bernard exclaims: "O, hard-hearted father! O cruel mother! O barbarous and impious parents! Yea not parents, but murderers, whose sorrows are the safety of their children; whose comfort, their destruction; who had rather that I should perish with them than reign with them. O strange abuse! The house is on fire, the flame singes my back, and when I am flying, I am forbidden to go out; when I am trying to escape, they persuade me to return. O fury! fie upon it. If you disregard your own death, why do you desire mine? If, I say, you care not for your own salvation, what does it avail you to oppose and prevent mine? What comfort is it to you to have me as associate of your damnation?"

The Council of Trent (18 Sess., 25 ch.) has pronounced anathema upon those who prevent young ladies from consecrating themselves to the service of God in the religious state. From this decree it is evident that the sin which parents or any one else commits against justice by unlawfully preventing one from becoming a religious, is so great that the punishment of excommunication may be inflicted upon them.

Many parents try to quiet their conscience by specious pretexts, saying for instance, that their son is too young and too unexperienced, that his pious sentiments are not the marks of a true voca-tion, that they must put him on trial, etc. The answer to these and similar pretexts is simply this, that God has not appointed parents for judges and interpreters of His holy will, concerning the sta'e of life which their children arc to embrace.—Unless parents are quite poor, let them not oppose their children in following the voice of God; let them not resemble Pharaoh, the King of Egypt, who tried to prevent the people of God from offering sacrifice to the Almighty in the Desert. Let them remember how the Lord punished this wicked King by drown-ing him and his whole army in the Red Sea.

Let them also remember what happened to Heli, the high priest, and to his sons, Ophni and Phinees. Holy Scripture tells us that ''the sin of Heli's sons was exceedingly great before the Lord, because they withdrew the people from the sacrifice of the Lord.'' (I. Kings 2, 17.) In punishment for their sin, they were slain in battle, and their father Heli who did not duly correct them, ''fell from his chair back-wards by the door, and broke his neck and died.'' (Chapt. IV, 18.)

Holy Scripture also tells us, how Moses one day sent twelve spies to reconnoitre the land of promise. Ten of these men, at their return, spoke ill of the land, in order to prevent the people of God from trying to take possession of it. In punishment for their sin, God struck them suddenly dead. Now, if God acted so severely towards those who deterred His people from His sacrifice, or from occupying an earthly country which He had promised them, how much more severely will He not act towards all those who oppose His chosen vessels of election in the passage to the religious state,—that truly earthly Paradise and the vestibule of heaven,—that there they may sacrifice their lives to the Lord and be His forever! Indeed, God is not slow in punishing those parents who prevent their children from sacrificing to Him their lives in the religious state. He either calls such parents, or their children out of this life by a premature death, or He inflicts on them different kinds of the most frightful temporal calamities, permitting, in many instances, the children of such parents, to become their most cruel scourge even in this life.

One day our Lord spoke to Mary Lataste, a holy sister of the Sacred Heart, in the following manner: "I am not come to bring peace on the earth, but division. The son will rise up against the father on account of Me, and the father against the son, and the mother against the daughter. You understand Me, my daughter, you will find no contradiction between these words and other teaching, that I have given you, at other times. I am come on the earth to direct towards heaven the minds of men who are crawling on the earth. My grace works in their hearts in the same sense. And very often, there are souls so filled and penetrated with My grace that nothing attaches them to earthly things, and they would abandon all, forget all, to be with Me alone. There are others, who leave the common ways of Christians to follow others more elevated, and which bring them nearer Me. Between these inclinations of grace and nature is found the division that I am come to bring in the world. I divide the movements of nature, and the movements of grace; I divide those who follow the movements of grace, and those who, on the other hand, are directed only by the movements of nature.

"There is a division among them, as between the heavens and earth, and the world and Me. There is a division between the child that I call to the sacerdotal state, and the father who destines for him the heritage of his ancestors. There is a division between the daughter, who has chosen Me for spouse, and the mother who wishes a marriage of flesh and blood, and not an alliance spiritual and divine between Me and her child. There is a division!! If you knew the effects of that division! If you could see the struggles between these senseless parents and the hearts of their children between these blind parents and the will of their children; between these

5*

carnal parents and their children sustained by My grace! Happy the children who do not allow themselves to be governed by the voice of father or mother in such circumstances, but rather listen to My voice! Their resistance rouses the anger of their family; but because they obey My call, they will become for their family a source of benediction. Wo, on the contrary, three times wo, forever wo, to the parents who turn their children from the way to which I call them, to plunge them into the world, into sin, and into hell! My daughter, there is no abomination that is not committed sometimes in this regard! You would tremble like a leaf in the tempest if I should reveal to you the multiplied infanticides that I know! Oh! fathers and mothers, unworthy of this name, who rob their children of an eternal for a temporal heritage; who rob their children of the joys of grace to give them the remorse of crime who rob them of the peace of a good conscience to give them the tortures of a soul, steeped in iniquity; who rob them of the liberty of the children of God to load them with the heavy chains of the sons of Belial. Oh! why have you engendered them, depraved fathers! Why have not your wombs remained sterill, mothers without heart? Fathers, why have you not sooner plunged a poniard in the heart of your children? Mothers, why have you not stifled in the cradle the fruit of your womb? If, at least, you had exposed them in a public place, where the passers-by would have received them! If you had thrown them into the waters of a river, where the bathers would have preserved them in their arms! But no! you have plunged them in iniquity; you have given them up to the world, to their passions, to Satan! Wo, wo to you! I have said, when I was on the earth, it would be better for such an one were a mill-stone on his neck and he should be thrown into the sea, than to scandalize one of My little ones. What shall I say of fathers and mothers who are not scandalized by their children, but who become their most cruel enemies, and bury them, so to speak, alive, night and day, in vice, instead of allowing them their right to practise virtue and give themselves to Me! Ah! such as these perform not the office of fathers and mothers, but the office of Satan! How much I pity these children, and how much I feel for their interest! Ah! if they had been always faithful in casting their eyes on Me! If they knew how to call Me to their succor! If they would hope in Me, nothing would repulse them, nothing stop them. They would forget their father and mother, to think only of their Father in heaven. They would not fear the father who could kill the body, but the Father who can throw them forever in the flames of hell.

How I deplore the blindness of these parents! It is God who demands their children, and they say to God Thou shalt not have our children. It is God who has bestowed them, and God must not have the right to demand them, to take them in His service, and pour on them special benedictions! Is not God, the first father of these children? Has He not rights superior to those of earthly parents? Is it just for them to dispute them? Is it just towards God, toward the children, not only to induce them not to give themselves to God, but, in reality, to prevent them from doing so. Ah! if they knew how to comprehend their interests! If an earthly king should demand their daughter in marriage, would they not esteem it a pleasure and honor to grant this request? Would they not consider such an alliance as a great honor to their family? But what is an earthly king compared with the King of heaven? This, however, is the idea of good with these parents! They prefer a sovereign of the earth to the great Sovereign of heaven and earth! What an outrage towards their God! What injustice towards Him! It is an outrage and an injustice towards their children; they are enlightened by a divine light, they see the truth, and wish to make themselves happy by embracing it, but are prevented from doing so by those who have given them birth. O blindness! O crime!

When monasteries were destroyed by wars, and the monks dispersed, it used to be holy Bishops who rebuilt them and collected again the separated brethren. Thus St. Amblardus, Archbishop of Lyons, when he found that the Norman ravages were probably at an end, rebuilt in a sumptuous style the abbey of Aisray.

Charles de Roucy, the venerable Bishop of Soissons, in 1582, counted it a great happiness in his last years, that he could favor the foundation of a new religious house in that city, in which Minims were to be received for the first time. Such were the works with which the holiest Bishops desired to close their administration.

Paul.—You are an unexperienced young man, and as such you see but the outside of the religious life, without understanding its true interior difficulties and hard obligations. You should then not contemplate taking such an important step now, but wait until you have reached a more mature age, in order not to entangle yourself in difficulties out of which you could not so easily extricate yourself.

Stanislas.—Can you foretell me with certainty that I shall reach such an age? Would to God that I had been fortunate enough to live in a monastery from my early childhood! Both our youth and old age belong to God and not to the world, and where, I ask, can young men whom you call unexperienced (and who, I add, are exposed to so many dangers) live with greater security, according to the maxims of the Gospel, than in religious institutes? A young man of the age of fifteen is commonly believed to be competent to judge rightly for himself. Were greater experience required, it would be rather as to how soon I should quit the world, than as to whether it be in itself expedient or not to embrace the evangelical counsels. For our Saviour Himself has exhorted us to His counsels, and has laid before us the excessive dangers and difficulties of a secular life. Besides, in religion I shall have a year or two of trial. I am not taking a leap in the dark, as do the greater part of those who marry. By one "yes" they contract marriage, which is indissoluble, and then make their Novitiate, which lasts for their whole life. They expected to have found a great treasure and it was but a rough stone; they hoped to live with a lamb and it was a lion or a poisonous snake. They soon shed bitter tears and exclaim: Had I known that, I would never have married; but in vain. Ask father and mother, whether I am right, and you will hear that I have said far too little on the subject. What I have seen of the world, and among married people, is enough to make me feel great compassion for the latter, and an utter disgust for the former. I need no more advice; mature reflection and good advice are needful in *doubtful affairs*; but not in that which regards the religious life, which is *certainly good*, because it is approved by the Holy Church and recommended by our Lord Himself in the Gospel.

Paul.—You cannot deny that there are many hard things in religion.

Stanislas —This is a gratuitous assumption and grave error, fraught with much evil, as it deters many from following the counsel of our Saviour. I grant that there are some hard things in religion. But what sort of life would it be, if nothing were to be suffered in it, if it had not now and then a dash of trouble. Were such the case, what commendation could it have? How could patience, fortitude, charity and other virtues be exercised? What occasion of merit could it afford? The religious life, is therefore, the more commendable, because it has wherein to practise virtue. But all the difficulty is so tempered and alloyed with comforts, that the labor is not felt; the goodness of God having so seasoned the matter, that what would in itself be hard, is wonderfully sweet and pleasant. But what need is there to defend the religious life in this point; as if the votaries of the world in whose behalf this objection is made, had nothing to suffer, no sorrow, no grief, whereas their sorrows and miseries and afflictions are a thousand times greater and more numerous. And being destitute of heavenly comfort, their troubles are the more intolerable. The slight causes of trouble in religion are easily removed, and they are sometimes such as it is better to despise or laugh at, or perhaps to love and willingly embrace; the comforts, on the other hand, are so abundant in our Saviour, as to be able to sweeten a whole sea of distastes and troubles, if any such were found in religion. For when wisdom has once bound a man, and tamed him with certain laborious exercises, it afterwards unbinds him, and gives him freedom to enjoy himself; and nurturing him first in temporal bonds, binds him afterwards with eternal embraces, than which bonds nothing can be imagined more delightful or more solid. The first bonds I confess are a little hard; of the second, I cannot say that they are hard, because they are sweet; nor soft, because they are strong. Whereas the bonds of this world have in them true harshness, false delight, uncertain pleasure, hard labor, timorous quiet, the thing itself full of misery, and a deceitful hope of happiness. I will beware of thrusting my neck, my hands and my feet into these fetters.

Paul.—But a life in common is certainly too hard for your constitution; you will soon break down, and be a corpse. Weak and delicate as you are, how will you be able to carry the burden of so hard a life?

says St. Jerome, "with her hair loose about her ears, and tearing her clothes, show you her breasts at which she nursed you; though your father lay himself down upon the threshold, pass them by, with dry eyes, in order to hasten to the standard of the Cross. A day will come hereafter when you shall enter the heavenly Jerusalem crowned like a man that has been valiant."

Paul.—But is it not to have a breast of iron and a heart of stone to leave parents in this way?

Stanislas.—Indeed, Paul, it is not; to be immoveable in this, is to be truly pious. If my parents believe in Christ, let them be on my side, when I go to fight for Christ; if they believe not in Him, "*then let the dead bury their dead.*"

To prefer the will of another to the will of God would be an infinite wrong to our Lord, and what punishment does not he deserve who prefers a creature to his Creator, darkness to light, dirt and ashes to heaven? "He is not worthy of Me." Nothing can fall heavier upon man than to be rejected as unworthy of the company of his God.

It is for this reason that several saints, when called to leave the world, quitted the house of their parents without even making their design known to them; thus did St. Francis Xavier, St. Philip Neri, St. Lewis Beltrando, St. Thomas Aquinas. Let me tell you what this great Doctor of the Church had

6

to suffer from his kindred for embracing the religious life. The frequent conversations which Thomas had with a Dominican Father, a very interior holy man, filled his heart with heavenly devotion and comfort, and inflamed him daily with a more and ardent love of God, which so burned in his breast that at his prayers his countenance seemed one day, as it were, to dart rays of light, and he conceived a vehement desire to consecrate himself wholly to God in that Order. His tutor perceived his inclinations and informed his father, the Count of Aquino, of the matter, who omitted neither threats nor promises to defeat such a design. But the saint, not listening to flesh and blood in the call of heaven, demanded with earnestness to be admitted into the Order, and accordingly received the habit in the Convent of Naples in 1243, being then seventeen years old. The Countess Theodora, his mother, being informed of it, set out for Naples to disengage him, if possible, from that state of life. Her son, on the first news of her journey, begged his Superiors to remove him, as they did first, to the Convent of St. Sabina in Rome, and soon after to Paris, out of the reach of his relations. Two of his brothers, Landulph and Reynold, commanders in the emperor's army in Tuscany, by her direction, so well guarded all the roads that he fell into their hands, near Acquapendente. They endeavored to pull off his habit, but he resisted them so violently that they conducted him in it to the seat of his parents, called Rocca Secca. The mother, overjoyed at their success, made no doubt of overcoming her son's resolution. She endeavored to persuade him that to embrace such an Order, against his parents, advice, could not be the call of heaven; adding all manner of reasons, fond caresses, entreaties and tears. Nature made her eloquent and pathetic. He appeared sensible of her affliction, but his constancy was not to be shaken. His answers were modest and respectful, but firm. He explained that his resolution was the call of God, and that it ought, consequently, to take place of all other views as to the disposition to be made of him even should these views aim at the service of God in any other way. At last, offended at his unexpected resistance, his mother expressed her displeasure in very angry words, and ordered him to be more closely confined and guarded, and that no one should see him but his two sisters. The reiterated solicitations of the young ladies were a long and violent assault. They omitted nothing that flesh and blood could inspire on such an occasion, and represented to him the danger of causing the death of his mother by grief. He, on the contrary, spoke to them in so moving a manner, on the contempt of the world, and the love of virtue, that they both yielded to the force of his reasons for quitting the world, and, by his persuasion, devoted themselves to a sincere practice of piety.

This solitude furnished him with the most happy opportunity for holy contemplation and assiduous prayer.

Some time after, his sisters conveyed to him some books, viz : a Bible, Aristotle's logic, and the works of the Master of the Sentences. During this interval his two brothers, Landulph and Reynold, returning home from the army, found their mother in the greatest affliction, and the young novice triumphant in his resolution. They would needs undertake to overcome him, and began their assault by shutting him up in a tower of the castle. They tore in pieces his habit on his back, and after bitter reproaches and dreadful threats, they left him, hoping his confinement, and the mortifications which every one strove to give him, would shake his resolution. This not succeeding, the devil suggested to these two young officers a new artifice for diverting him from pursuing his vocation. They secretly introduced one of the most beautiful and most insinuating young strumpets of the country into his chamber, promising her a considerable reward in case she could draw him into sin. She employed all the arms of Satan to succeed in so detestable a design. The saint, alarmed and affrighted at the danger, profoundly humbled himself, and **cried out** to God most earnestly for his protection; then snatching up a fire-brand struck her with it, and drove her out of his chamber. After this victory, not moved with pride, but blushing with confusion for having been so basely assaulted, he fell on his knees and thanked God for his merciful preservation, consecrated to Him anew his chastity and redoubled his prayers, and the earnest cry of his heart, with sighs and tears, to obtain the grace of being always faithful to his promises. Then falling into a slumber, as the most ancient historians of his life relate, he was visited by two angels, who seemed to gird him round the waist with a cord so tight that it awaked him, and made him cry out. His guards ran in, but he kept his secret to himself. It was only a little before his death that he disclosed this incident to Father Reynold, his confessor, adding that he had received this favor about thirty years before, from which time he had never been annoyed with temptations of the flesh; yet he constantly used the utmost caution and watchfulness against that enemy, and he would otherwise have deserved to forfeit that great grace. One heroic victory sometimes obtains of God a recompense and triumph of this kind. Our saint having suffered in silence this imprisonment and persecution upwards of a twelvemonth, some say two years, at length, on the remonstrances of Pope Innocent IV., and the

6*

emperor Frederick, on account of so many acts of violence in his regard, both the countess and his brothers began to relent. The Dominicans of Naples being informed of this, and that his mother was disposed to connive at measures that might be taken to procure his escape, they hastened in disguise to Rocca Secca, where his sisters, knowing that the countess no longer opposed his escape, contrived his being let down out of his tower in a basket. He was received by his brethren in their arms, and carried with joy to Naples. The year following he there made his profession, looking on that day as the happiest of his whole life in which he made a sacrifice of his liberty that he might belong to God alone. But his mother and brothers renewed their complaints to Pope Innocent IV., who sent for Thomas to Rome, and examined him on the subject of his vocation to the state of religion, in their presence; and having received entire satisfaction on this head, the Pope admired his virtue, and approved of his choice of that state of life, which from that time he was suffered to pursue in peace.

By following the example of such great Saints, we cannot err, especially if we consider that the Lord showed by miracles that He approved their glorious flight. St. Peter of Alcantara, in going from the house of his mother (to whom he had always paid the strictest obedience since the death of his father), to the monastery in which he was about to become a religious, found his flight impeded by a large river, which he did not know how to cross. He recommended himself to God, and was, in an instant, miraculously transported to the opposite side. So, in a similar case, Stanislas Kostka, when fleeing from his home, without his father's permission, was closely followed by his brother in a carriage, with the object of capturing him; but, just as he was on the point of doing so, the horses stopped suddenly, and could not be made to advance; but, after a short resistance wheeled round and quickly proceeded back to the town. We have also the example of the Blessed Oringa of Valdorno in Tuscany, who, being promised by her parents in marriage to a young man, fled from him to consecrate herself to God; but finding her way stopped by the river Arno, she prayed for a few moments to God, whereupon the waters opened, and rising on each side like two crystal walls, afforded her a dry passage.

It is, therefore, not necessary to seek the counsel or the consent of our parents to our compliance with our vocation. The tenth Council of Toledo, in the last chapter, says expressly, that children may become religious without the consent of their parents, provided they are past the age of puberty. These are the words of the Council: "Parents will not devote their children to religion unless they are under fourteen years of age. After this period it is for children to follow their own wishes in this respect, either with the consent of their parents, or according to their own devotion, independently of the direction of parents." The same rule is prescribed by the Council of Tiber (Can. 24), and it is taught by St. Ambrose, St. Jerome, St. Augustine, St. Bernard, St. Thomas, and others, as well as by St. John Chrysostom, who says in his General Thesis, that when parents oppose what regards the spiritual welfare of their children, they must cease to be regarded on that point as parents.

Paul admired the acuteness of his brother's mind, and felt perplexed, as it were, at the wise answers which he made to his objections. In his heart he was convinced that Stanislas, after all, was right; but he could not as yet give up the hope that he would succeed at last in dissuading his brother from embracing the religious life; so he thought of other objections.

Paul.—You are right Stanislas, but remember, that the duties of religious are far more difficult than those of seculars, and that the weakness of the will is far greater than that of the body. This is a point worthy of consideration. How often do we not propose to ourselves good things, and afterwards find out that we cannot accomplish them.

Stanislas.—Rich people, it is true, have to pay more taxes than the poor, yet, for all that, the former are better off than the latter, for they have more means to comply with their duties. So in religion; even granted that religious had to perform harder and more numerous duties than seculars have, yet, for all that, they are better off. God knows our misery and our weakness, and yet He invites us to take upon ourselves His yoke and His burden. Those who follow His invitation are assisted by His grace, and thus His yoke becomes sweet and His burden light. Let me explain. Every man has a natural and inbred inclination and propensity to virtue, manifesting itself in the joy which he experiences within himself when he does well, and on the other hand, the sadness and defection of mind when he does amiss. If nature therefore be inclined to virtue, the practice of it must needs be more or less easy and pleasant; though this inclination to virtue has been much weakened by original sin, and the multitude of our own offences; yet these are but outward incumbrances, as clouds between us and the sun or as ashes heaped upon the embers; inwardly nature still inclines to virtue and a good life, and reason always inclines us that way whenever these outward impediments happen to be removed. This kind of inclination or facility of doing good has been implanted by God in our very nature;

but it is nothing in proportion to that which the force of His grace gives us. That which is in nature is but a beginning, a kind of seed, which of itself alone can do nothing. Grace gives the true form and soul, as it were, out of which virtuous actions proceed; and makes a man, a *new man*, celestial and divine, and gives a new heart, and "*reneweth an upright spirit within us.*"

Besides that grace which God offers to all to do good, the peculiar grace of a religious vocation puts so much life and strength into those who have it, that they perform with great facility, and in a manner without any labor at all, all those things which others cannot do, and which they themselves could not do before. A beast which has no reason cannot perform anything that belongs to and proceeds from reason, such as to draw a conclusion, to judge of a thing, to give advice, to foresee that which is to come; but a man, being endowed with reason, does these things as easily and promptly as he uses his hands or feet. So if a man has not the vocation and spirit of God, which includes poverty and obedience and other virtues, he finds it very hard to be content to have nothing, and to do the will of another; but if he has this vocation, he takes great comfort and delight in the performance of all his duties.

Moreover, the practice breeds a habit of doing

well, and when this practice is once settled in the mind, all virtuous actions are easy and pleasant. The affection which excludes earthly love is strenghened by the custom of well-doing ; because a man's conscience must necessarily take delight in good works and willingly do that which it is glad it has done. Therefore, religion being nothing else but a continual practice in all kinds of virtue, the exercise of it must needs grow easier every day, and in time bring forth abundant fruit. When a man has once acquired a perfect habit of practising virtue, and is advanced in love for it, so as to consider it the most precious thing in the world, and to look upon vice, or the poison of sin, as the greatest torment, he takes more pleasure in his sober and continent life than others do in their incontinence and riot; the flower of chastity must needs be sweeter to him than the filth of sensual pleasure to the sensual; and finally, when he is humbled and meets with an occasion to suffer for Jesus Christ, he rejoices more in his humiliation and sufferings than worldly, ambitious people do in the applause and preferments after which they run so eagerly.

I therefore say, that the duties of the religious life, so far from being more irksome and more difficult than those of secular people, are rather wonderfully sweet and pleasant. St. Reginaldus, one of the first companions of St. Dominic, was a wealthy man in the world and lived daintily at his ease. After he had become a religious, those who knew him before often asked him whether his present life was not rather hard for him; and he always replied with a cheerful heart and countenance: "I wish you to know that all these things are so sweet and pleasant to me, that I have often thought that I merit nothing in my present life, because I find so much comfort and joy in it." All good religious, if asked, would make the same answer.

Paul.—Dear Stanislas, you cannot deney that there have been many who, full of zeal for their perfection, overcame the greatest obstacles in order to become religious, and who, after they had received the religious habit, would have suffered themselves to be cut to pieces rather than give up one inch of their habit. But how long did their fervor last? Alas! they soon grew lukewarm, and to their great confusion, left the Order, and endangered their salvation more than before; nay, among those who already have taken the vows many can be found who speak in disparagement of the religious life.

Stanislas.—There are a great many seculars who speak very contemptuously of the world, and would be too glad if they could leave it. But why do you not leave it as there is nothing to prevent you from doing so? The fact that many have become unfaithful in the service of God, and thereby endangered their salvation more than before, must not deter us from doing what is good and perfect. Otherwise it would be wrong for a man to speak to a Turk, or a Jew, or a heathen, of the true Christian religion, for fear that, after his conversion, he might lead a bad life, and bring upon himself greater punishments for all eternity. How many soldiers have not lost their lives on the battle-field? How many merchants have not become bankrupt? How many have not perished by shipwreck, and by railroad accidents? and yet for all that men are not deterred from travelling by sea and by land; from becoming soldiers or men of business. Shall we give up working out our salvation and striving to attain one day to the kingdom of heaven because one-third of the angels were driven out of it and became devils? Assuredly, to yield to the suggestions of the apostate angels would be very wrong; but would it not be just as wrong to allow ourselves to be prevented from embracing a holy course of life by the examples of apostate religious? Some of them, it is true, speak contemptuously of the religious state; they do so to justify their conduct in the eyes of men, and if possible, to quiet their conscience, not foreseeing that by so doing, they render their case worse before God and men. Their unfaithfulness does not prove that the religious state is not a holy state, a hidden treasure; it does not

5

prove that the promises of Christ are not true. Oh no! it proves only that the grace of a religious vocation is not granted in such a manner that it cannot be forfeited; it proves that after we have put the hand to the plough, we must not look back; it proves that the kingdom of heaven must be carried by violence even in religion. The very fact that those who have left the Orders to which they belonged feel unhappy, shows that they are guilty; for a man with a good conscience feels always happy. We must, then, never look at the examples of the bad. Their conduct must never inspire us with immoderate fear. The greater part of the angels were faithful and stayed in heaven; so also the greater part of religious persevere in their holy vocation and die as Saints. Alas! how necessary is it not for us to put all our confidence in God in order to persevere in our good resolutions! Let us rest assured that He who inspires good resolutions, and specially that of embracing the religious life, will also give strength to persevere in it. But we must constantly ask for it. "Whatsoever you ask the Father in My name, you shall receive."

Paul.—I know, from reliable persons that, even in Religious Orders, there are some who do not live well; and you know the proverb: "One scabby sheep infects a whole flock." Why, then, should you go amongst them and be infected and lose your innocence?

Stanislas.—What a strange objection this! Is it right to charge the innocent with the fault of the guilty, or what is worse, to impute it to the state itself, which is the work of God? No wonder, if men speak ill of the servants of the Lord and labor to stain their reputation, when they cannot deprave their life! Some people have strange notions of religious men, as if, with their state, they had at once changed their nature, and were no longer men of the common clay. If they see them attend to the necessities of their body, they load them with reproaches and slanders, and turning their calumnies from one upon all, they call them gluttons, forgetful of the manner in which they themselves feast daily, and the shameful excesses in food and drink in which they not unfrequently indulge. But even granted that some religious have sometimes their faults, is the religious state itself on that account, to be censured? Is all money bad because there is some counterfeit? Should there be some who are not good, let them alone. Let us not cast our eyes upon Judas denying his Lord, but upon Paul confessing Him. As the light of the stars disappears in that of the sun, so the blemishes of some religious disappear in the light of the bright examples of the multitude of their brethren who are models of every virtue. Nowhere are there more mangy sheep than in the world. In religion they are the rare exceptions.   Nor will they be suffered to remain long among the virtuous.   They will soon amend, or, if they do not, they will leave, of their own accord, or be expelled, and the good and fervent alone remain.   If some of the angels in heaven, if Adam and Eve in Paradise, could rebel against God, shall a sensible man be astonished to learn that now and then a religious forgets himself.   If there is danger everywhere, is it reasonable to choose to stay where the danger is the greatest?

Paul.—But the sins of religious people are more grievous than the sins of those who live in the world, and consequently deserve greater punishments. Why, then, expose yourself to the danger of making yourself more guilty and damnable?

Stanislas.—If what you say were true, the case of religious would be rather hard.   But the contrary, is true.   If a religious commit a fault, it is not from habit and custom, but from a sudden motion. Now, such a fault is comparatively of little moment, because it does not proceed from a depraved will. But the faults of secular people springing, as they generally do, from sinful habits are evidence of a will more confirmed in evil, and consequently deserve a greater punishment.   Moreover, as a good father scarcely takes notice of the faults of a child that tries to be good, so God easily forgives the faults of religious who try to please Him by all they do.

Their faults are swallowed up in the good they do, and their good deeds are a constant prayer for mercy. "And therefore," said the prophet to King Josaphat, "thou didst deserve indeed the wrath of God, but good works have been found in thee."

Again, a religious person has more knowledge of God and often remembers Him, so that He cannot so carelessly cast himself away and plunge so deep into sin as people in the world generally do, because they know God but little and live in forgetfulness of His Divine Majesty. Hence it is said in Holy Writ: "A just man, when he falleth, shall not be bruised."

Besides, religious persons know how to profit by their faults, as St. Peter did by his. If now and then they happen to present withered roses—imperfect actions—to our Lord, they learn how to press out of them the odoriferous water of compunction or the wholesome oil of humility.

Paul.—But is it not said that "to whom much is given of him much shall be required"

Stanislas.—He Who said this said also that "he who hath, to him shall be given, and he shall abound." Jesus Christ, no doubt, will demand much of all Christians; yet it is peculiar to Almighty God to enrich still more those upon whom He has already heaped so many spiritual and temporal blessings, and we may say, in truth, that it concerns

5*

Him much to have an eye to religious, and to strengthen and establish them in what He gave them in the beginning of their vocation, lest they lose it. He never bestows His gifts, especially the grace of a religious vocation for our greater ruin, but for our greater profit and happiness. Those who, from such an ungrounded fear, or any other reason, do not like to receive the grace of a religious vocation, or reject it altogether when offered by Almighty God, resemble the unprofitable servant in the Gospel, and will with him, *"tied hand and foot, be cast into utter darkness."* As it is easy for a rich man to profit by his wealth and acquire a greater abundance of it, so it is also very easy for religious to profit by the great gifts of God and increase their spiritual wealth. It is also to be observed here that religious in their state are not bound to be perfect, but they are only bound to aspire to perfection. Those who think otherwise are entirely mistaken. Religious comply with this duty if they keep themselves in the way towards perfection. It is not required of a scholar that he be learned all at once; he is required only to try to learn his lesson as well as he is able. The same may be said of religious persons; if they do not wholly cast aside the thought of virtue, but if they, with proper care and diligence, labor to acquire it, they cannot be said to fail in their duty; and those very steps towards virtue, though short, bring them nearer and nearer to God, Who, far from overloading them, lays rather less upon them than they are able to do. We may therefore say with joy what we find in Holy Writ: "Our Lord will be merciful to all who, with their whole heart, seek the Lord the God of their fathers, and will not impute it to them that they are less sanctified."

Paul.—Stanislas, you seem to be filled with a great desire of perfection. You ought, then, to have a good opportunity to acquire a large treasure of merits. This opportunity is given you in the practice of mortification and in the hard labors for the salvation of your neighbor. But in religion you cannot have this opportunity as often as you wish, because your superiors will often interfere.

Stanislas.—The true and only source of merit is the will of God. Only those actions, which are done according to His will, are blessed and rewarded. Now, where is the will of God better manifested and more perfectly done than in religion? To every action of a religious a double merit is attached, that of the good action itself and that of obedience.

Besides, God has established every religious Society for a particular end. To obtain this end, God gives it a particular grace. Every religious, when laboring for the welfare of his neighbor, has from God a twofold grace, that which is common to all good men when employed in such good works, and also that grace which God gives to the Society to reach its end. For these reasons it is that the labors of religious are so much blessed everywhere. There have been persons who attributed the admirable results of the Apostolic labors in which they were employed to their own talents and efforts; they thought they could do more good if they enjoyed full liberty and were not hindered by obedience due to superiors. Deceived by a most fatal error, and their pride of heart, they regarded the fountain of Divine benediction as an impediment, and ascribed to their own natural and acquired talents the efficiency which was in truth imparted to them as living members of a Religious Society. But no sooner had these religious left their Order, than they found that they were destitute of this efficiency, and that the success of their labors was reduced to the common level, and sometimes scarcely attained to mediocrity.

"A religious, therefore, "says St. Alphonsus, "will save, by his prayers, labors and mortifications, more souls in one year, than in his whole life out of religion; and as to his own personal merit, he will gain more in one year by practising obedience than in ten years by living in the world according to his own will."

Paul.—But it seems to me, Stanislas, that by

embracing the religious life you are acting uncharitably towards your own kindred, neighbors and countrymen; you withdraw from them your good example, and your zeal to advance them in a virtuous life, and you bestow all that upon strangers. This cannot be according to the will of God; it cannot but displease Him, and we are bound in duty to be more good to our own kindred than to strangers.

Stanislas.—True charity is well ordered ; if it is not, it is not charity, but some other affection which puts on the mask of charity. "Charity commences at home," that is, every one must first be careful of himself and prefer his own spiritual benefit and profit, to that of any neighbor. Now, the greatest profit and advantage to ourselves is the acquisition of the possession of God. He is the greatest good of our soul. The acquisition of this good is nowhere sooner and more solidly made and preserved than in religion. Hence, the course of a religious life is, beyond doubt, the most absolute course of our own perfection and far more apt to furnish our own souls with virtue, than can any secular state whatever. From this necessarily follows, that, though some particular state in the world might be more beneficial to our neighbor, yet the good of our own souls is to be preferred. Our Saviour tells us so in these express words: "What doth it profit a man if he gain the whole world and suffer the loss of his own soul." Hence, in the matter of salvation and sanctification no degree of compassionate charity is to be preferred to that degree which the Wise man sets down, when he says: "Have mercy on thy own soul, pleasing God." But a religious life, as I have already said, is far better calculated to do good to others than a life in the world; for every one knows that the conversion of souls, their progress and advancement in virtue depends entirely on the grace of God. Men are but instruments which God uses. Hence a man will do good to his neighbor in proportion as he is united with God, and moved by Him; so far he will go, and no further.

Now there can be no question as to who is more united with God, a man in the world, or a man in religion. The religious man being given over absolutely, and bound inseparably to God, by his vows, placed as a staff in His hands, to be ruled and wielded by Him as He pleases, what wonder if such an instrument, managed by the hand of so great and so skillful a Master, and so fit and pliable to His hand, should work such rare and admirable effects as are visible in the church of God. And as for expecting to do more good by remaining to instruct our kindred, neighbors, or countrymen, than by going into religion, Jesus Christ Himself tells us: "A prophet is not without power except in his own country." But not only our Lord's words, but even His own example prove the same; for even amongst the Samaritans, though a debauched kind of people, all admired His wisdom; yet in His own country He was held in contempt and derision, so much so that it is said in the Gospel: "He could not there do any virtue." What, then, can we, weak and infirm creatures as we are, expect to do, seeing that the infinite sanctity and majesty of our Lord Himself could effect no good upon flesh and blood. Whoever wishes to save a man from being drowned, must first put himself in safety; otherwise he endangers himself in the attempt. In like manner, he who will go about to help his neighbor out of the danger which is in the world must wade out of the world, and stand upon firm ground above all worldly things.

Paul.—Stanislas, you know but too well what value Jesus Christ sets upon alms-deeds. On the day of the last judgment, He will not ask His creatures whether they have entered into religion, nor praise them for having done so, but to those who have been very charitable towards the poor He will say: "I was hungry, and you gave Me to eat; I was thirsty, and you gave Me to drink; I was naked, and you clothed Me." Now, if you enter into religion, you have to renounce all the goods of this world; you can no longer dispose of them as you please, and thus rob yourself of the best opportunity of doing good. You act, then, very unwisely by leaving us.

Stanislas.—There seems to be some plausible reason in what you have just said; I must avow that this very consideration made me one day waver in my resolution. But. thanks to Divine Providence, a little book which at the time I happened to read . dispersed all my doubts on the subject. Let me tell you what I remember still.

1. Vigilantius maintained, that those who give their possessions little by little to the poor, do better than those who sell them and give all away at once. This proposition is heretical and condemned by the church. For Jesus Christ Himself has declared: "If you wish to be perfect, go and sell all you have and give to the poor and follow Me." It is far better to give the tree together with the fruits at once, than the fruits only little by little. Were God to give you all the goods of this world, your heart would not feel so contented and so happy, as it would were He to bestow Himself whole and entire upon your soul. In the same manner he who gives alms, gives to Christ his earthly goods; but he who becomes a religious, consecrates to God his whole person, and gives at once the tree with the fruits, and this offering is far more pleasing to His Divine Majesty. Hence it is that on the day of

judgment, Jesus Christ will say to the alms-givers: "Come, ye blessed of My Father, possess the kingdom, etc., for I was hungry and ye gave Me to eat," etc. But those who for Christ's sake have renounced all things, will be higher than the alms-givers, for they will be their judges, according to the promise of our Lord: "Amen, I say to you, that you who have forsaken all things and followed Me, in the regeneration, when the Son of man shall sit in His Majesty, you shall also sit upon twelve seats judging the twelve Tribes of Israel."

2. The members of Religious Orders give alms through the hands of their Superiors.

3. No acts of charity are so pleasing in the sight of God as laboring for the salvation of souls. "We cannot offer any sacrifice to God," says St. Gregory, "which is equal to that of the zeal for the salvation of souls." "This zeal and labor," says St. John Chrysostom, "is of so great a merit before God, that to *give up all our goods to the poor*, or to *spend our whole life* in the exercise of all sorts of austerities, cannot equal the merit of this labor. This merit of laboring in the vineyard of the Lord is something far greater, than the gift of working miracles. To be employed in this blessed labor is even more pleasing to the Divine Majesty than to suffer martyrdom." Religious, then, who devote their whole life to this most glorious labor in the vineyard of

6

the Lord, have undoubtedly chosen the best kind of meritorious works.

4. If in the opinion of the Fathers of the Church there can be no greater merit than that of working for the salvation of souls, we must also say, that there can be no work of corporal mercy more meritorious, than that of giving charitable aid to Religious Societies, whose members are consecrated to the service of God and their neighbor. Now, let me suppose, I were to labor hard from morning to night and give all the income of the industry of my whole life in support of such a Society, you would certainly say that I could not go farther in my charity. But I can and I will go one step farther; I can and I will be still more generous and liberal by entering into such a Society, and being industrious there according to obedience. Thus all my labors and exertions will prove as so many alms to the Order, and have at the same time the merit and reward of obedience.

5. Were I to stay in the world, I should have to spend a large portion of the income of my labors for the necessaries of life. In religion, I can live much cheaper, and thus more of the income of my industry goes to the noblest of purposes.

6. In the world different societies are organized to carry out great plans for making much money, which otherwise could not be carried out for want

of means; and the stockholders of such societies soon become very rich. In like manner, Religious Societies are established by Almighty God to carry out the plans of His wisdom for the salvation of mankind. Every religious is a stockholder in the Society, and shares in all the spiritual gains which the Society makes in the vineyard of the Lord. Let me also remark, that if a society organized for worldly purposes, should fail, its stockholders would suffer great loss. Such a risk is not to be apprehended in religion. The establishment of a Religious Society being the work of God, can never fail. The Lord will always give it the necessary means to carry out His plans. My gains are in the most reliable insurance company—Jesus Christ is its President, and has given me a good Policy recorded in the Gospel in these words : "He who shall leave his home, brothers, or sisters, or father, or mother, or wife, or children, or estate, for My sake, shall receive a hundred-fold in this life, and eternal life hereafter in the world to come." (Matt. xix., 29.) "Heaven and earth shall pass away, but My word shall not pass away." (Matt. xxiv., 53.) May the Lord be blessed for having enlightened me so much on this subject.

Paul.—In your estimation, the religious life is all, and the life led in the world is nothing; in the latter, men have to suffer far more tribulations.

than religious.   Married people especially may, in truth, be called martyrs, for I assure you, the greater part of them suffer as much, and perhaps more, than many a martyr of the Church did.   I pass in silence the merit which parents acquire by the good education of their children; I will not mention the heroic fortitude required to preserve oneself innocent amidst the dangers of the world, and say in truth : "In the midst of the fire I was not burnt." (Eccl. li., 6.)

Stanislas.—What great blindness !   Were that so it would be necessary for the Church to constitute a new class of martyrs, which, of course, she will not do ; not only married people, but also soldiers who sacrifice their lives in war, would be martyrs. People who marry, says St. Paul, "shall have tribulation of the flesh."   (I. Cor. vii., 28.,) The greater part of them suffer so much because they wish to enjoy the pleasures of the flesh, and you think that they should be ranked among the martyrs.   The case is quite different with religious.   The holy Church says of St. Paula, who, as a widow, embraced the religious life, that she was *at last* crowned with the crown of a long martyrdom.   And the same may be said of every fervent religious who dies in his Order.

Paul.—And what do you say of the merit which parents acquire in the good education of their children ?   Am I not right in this point ?

Stanislas.—By no means, my dear brother; for the merit of a good education is far greater in religious than in parents; the children of the latter become the spiritual sons and daughters of religious who by their prayer, good example, advice and exhortations in the confessional and out of it, lead both parents and their children to life everlasting; thus religious have a greater number of spiritual children than parents have according to the flesh. For this reason St. Bernard exclaims: "The religious state fills heaven with angels."

Paul.—But is it not something great to know how to keep oneself guiltless amidst the dangers of the world?

Stanislas.—I know there are many people in the world who are good; nay, some of them may even be better than many a religious; but they are few in comparison, because few give their heart and soul to the service of God, and they may therefore be looked upon as the exception, not the rule; whereas, those who do so in religion, are the rule, the others the exception. This makes a great difference. In the point in question we must be guided by what commonly happens. I know the three children were not hurt in the fire, nor was Peter in the sea, and many others have on similar occasions escaped unhurt. But do you think that there is any one mad enough to cast himself wilfully into

6*

the sea, or into the fire, because these men escaped by the particular protection of God? So of the world; it is so deceitful. and so infested with sin, that it is hard for one to avoid committing it, and there are but few who escape it. Now, who can guarantee that I shall be one of the few? What folly, then, to transact a business of so much importance as our eternal salvation in a place where spiritual bankruptcy occurs so frequently, or to imagine that the poison of the world will have no effect upon me, though all admit that it has upon others. The holy King David says: "With the elect, thou wilt be elect, and with the perverse, thou wilt be perverted." (II. Kings, xxii., 27.)

Paul.—Granted that the works of piety in the world are not of so great a merit as those performed under religious obedience; this defect can easily be supplied by charity; "perfection," as St. Paul says, "consists in charity," so that the greater a man's charity, the greater is also his perfection, no matter whether he lives in the world or in religion. Witness Abraham, Isaac and Jacob, who, though living in the state of matrimony and abounding in worldly goods, were nevertheless holy in an eminent degree. Witness again Casimir, St. Henry the Emperor, St. Charles Borromeo, St. Francis de Sales and many others who are venerated on our altars, and who lived in the world and reached a most eminent degree of sanctity. Let a man, there-fore, forsake the world in affection and love God very much, and he will die a great Saint.

Stanislas.—It is true, perfection consists in charity, and the religious state is not perfection, but a way and means to it; yet a means so efficacious as most inevitably and easily leads to it; while on the other hand, those who do not embrace it, either never come to perfection, or not without long and most difficult efforts, as I have already explained.

As to the Patriarchs Abraham, Isaac and others of the Old Law, I hope, you do not wish me to put, like them, calves upon the altar of the Lord, and kill rams and sacrifice goats. We are living under a New Law, under the Law of Perfection, given by Jesus Christ. God requires more from us than from the Patriarchs of the Old Law. As men expect more at their childrens, hands when they are grown up than when they are children, and find fault with those things in elder years which it was a pleasure for them to see in their tender age: so God in those first times condescended in many things, which now, in the light of the Gospel, we see are imperfect, especially seeing that greater rewards are promised us, and that the grace of the Holy Ghost has been more abundantly poured upon us, and greater gifts bestowed by the coming of Christ, who, of weak and feeble creatures as we are, makes us perfect. The just of the Old Law walked in the depth of the divided sea, as it were, and in the mire of many waters, possessing earthly things, and that lawfully; but we have another more wonderful manner of walking upon the waters themselves, by forsaking all things: which state and prerogative was due to the state of the Gospel, and to St. Peter, as the leader and captain of it. We must, therefore, follow Jesus Christ, His example, and His doctrine. In conclusion, I must still remark that it would be great boldness and presumption to put ourselves on the same level with the Saints. If some of them have lived virtuously in the midst of their wealth and honor in either state of life, married or single, what reason have we to believe that we shall have the same degree of grace to live in the same humble spirit in which they lived? No man is so foolish as to attack a whole army of men by himself, without weapon, because he has heard that Samson slew so many of his enemies with no other weapon than the jaw-bone of an ass.

Paul.—You have brought forward many strong arguments in favor of the religious life; you have extolled its beauty and advantages in the plainest and most forcible manner. But I think, that there are but few religious who enjoy all those advantages. Pray, tell me, where in religion are those men who, with a blessed Ephraim, can exclaim :"O Lord, leave me a little, because the weakness of this vessel is not able to contain Thy sweetness," or with St. Francis Xavier : "It is enough, O Lord, it is enough."

Stanislas.—Whatever I have said of the beauty, excellence, benefit, or pleasure of the religious life, is to be understood of the state itself, not of particular men. In the discussion of the constitution of a man's body, we consider it as it is by nature, entire and perfect, and not as it may be found in some particular cases, deprived of a hand, or an eye, or a foot, or any other part. So, in religion, we show what profit and happiness the state is apt and wont naturally to produce and to afford. If there is any particular religious in whom it does not produce this usual effect the fault is in the individual, not in the state. However, the number of such slothful and idle people who suffer themselves to want in the midst of plenty, is very small if compared to those who take real comfort in religion, because it is one of the happinesses and benefits of the religious life to rouse up the spirits of such as are indolent and careless, and to infuse life into the dull and phlegmatic. As to those extraordinary favors which certain saints have received, I know that they do not happen to all. But it is no dishonor to religion, if all religious are not endowed with such extraordinary gifts. A piece of land may yield a hundred-fold to one farmer, whilst to another it yields far less. The quality of the soil is, of course, not to be blamed for this, but rather the negligence, or incapacity of him who tills it. So of the religious state ; of itself it is a very rich soil, whose fertility appears chiefly in the production of great Saints ; if it does not yield the hundred-foldto all, the fault is, more or less, in the individual, This consideration ought to encourage all religious to be more diligent and fervent in the performance of their duties. But there are other ordinary comforts of great value which all religious may easily obtain, provided they follow the common and ordinary manner of a religious life—comforts which are grounded in purity of heart and the practice of mortification.

As for myself, I know of no more solid comfort nor of any more ravishing delight than that of being certain of always doing the will of God. Jesus Christ said: "My food is to do the will of Him that sent Me." (Johniv.,34.) A religious always has the same food and may say in truth with St. Paul: "I live, now not I, but Christ liveth in me." (Gal.li.,20.) O what sweet comfort, what rapture in this thought! Again, is it not a constant comfort for a religious to have the firm, certain hope of everlasting happiness?—a comfort not transitory like the pleasures of the senses, but a life-long comfort, increasing in intensity in proportion to its duration.

The sun, as you know, is wont to communicate its light to every thing, according to the disposition of the thing itself; supposing, for instance, the air is pure, it is full of light; if cloudy and misty, it is not destitute of light, but receives as much as it is capable of receiving.

So does God deal with His servants. To generous and noble souls in whom He finds no obstacle, He communicates Himself profusely; others not so perfect He does not forsake, but gives them light and grace in proportion to the capacity of each.

The gifts and comforts of God are like the oil which was multiplied by the Prophet Elias; they run so long as there are empty vessels to receive them. Let us never fear or doubt, lest God should sell His spiritual delights at too dear a rate. He freely and profusely pours forth His benefits for the sustenance of our natural life; He showers down these benefits even upon those who blaspheme His holy Name and abuse His gifts, or at least are for the most part ungrateful; assuredly, He is not less liberal and profuse in the goods which serve to sustain our spiritual life; for the sake of these goods He voluntarily descended from heaven and died willingly upon the cross.

What kind of people does He invite to the sumptuous banquet so royally and magnificently set forth in the Gospel? "Go forth quickly," He says, "into the streets and lanes of the city ; and bring hither the poor, the blind and the lame." Who are those feeble, blind and poor people? Are they not the imperfect, or those who are but novices in the spiritual life? And these are not only not excluded from the sweetness of this banquet, but are unexpectedly invited, entreated, and as the Gospel says, *compelled to go in.* No one, therefore, who is called to the religious life, should fear that he will be kept fasting from those spiritual fruits of the religious state, or forced to labor too long in digging for this current of living water.

Christ has promised the hundred-fold not only to those who live like St. Arsenius, or St. Hilarion, but absolutely to *all* who forsake *all.* Therefore let no one say: I am of a tender complexion ; I am a sinner ; I cannot go through a course of hard labor and penances to deserve great graces. Is not grace always grace, that is, a gratuitous gift? Have not all sinned? Do you think there is exception of persons with God? And that, therefore, He does not so plentifully comfort all that have left all? Be not of such little faith ; believe the God of Truth when He says : "And every one that shall leave father, or mother, or house, or land for My name's sake, shall receive a hundred-fold." They, therefore, are miserable that say : "Christ, of course, excepts no man, *except us.*" I know these fears are generally those of beginners, though they have the least cause to entertain them. Indeed, it is so far from being true that these comforts are bestowed only upon the perfect, that sometimes they are bestowed more profusely upon the imperfect, and upon such as come as strangers into the house of God. The Lord deals with man like a tender father who watches more carefully over his sickly children than over those who enjoy good health. It is for this reason that Jesus Christ has said: "They that are in health need not a physician, but they that are sick."

Let us rest assured, that if St. Paul could say in truth, "I reckon, that the sufferings of this present time are not worthy to be compared with the glory to come, that shall be revealed in us," I am not wrong when I say, that the sufferings in the religious life are not worthy to be even compared with the advantages and graces which religious enjoy in their holy state. For of those who dwell in the House of God is always true what holy David said: "They shall be inebriated with the plenty of Thy house, and Thou shalt make them drink of the torrent of Thy pleasure."

Now, my dear brother Paul, I hope all your difficulties in embracing the religious life are removed. I hope that God, in the course of our conversation, has enkindled in your heart a great desire to conse-

7

crate yourself to His service in the religious state, and that you will not resemble the young man in the Gospel, who went away sorrowful from our Lord, when invited to a life of perfection in these words: "If thou wilt be perfect, go, sell what thou hast, and give to the poor, and thou shalt have treasure in heaven, and come follow Me." (Matt. xix., 21.)

Paul.—Indeed, my dear brother Stanislas, your words made a deep impression upon me. I feel convinced that you are right in all that you have said. I feel a rather strong desire to follow your example,—but I hesitate a little, not knowing for certain whether this desire is inspired by God, and a sign of His will that I should be a religious. I have known certain young persons who had the strongest desire and the best of motives to become religious, and yet could never succeed. Who does, then, not see how difficult it is to know whether such desires are inspired by God and to be followed?

Stanislas.—This is a question rather difficult for me to answer. But let me tell you the reply to it, which I heard one day from a holy priest and religious. St. Thomas, said he, puts the question: what is it in a soul that first and principally moves it? and he answers, that Reason first moves all other parts and powers of it, and that which moves Reason, is some thing better than reason; it is not knowl-

edge or learning, for these are not better than
reason, but it is God; and the holy Doctor adds,
that they whom God moves to embrace the religious
life, need not take further advice on the matter, because they are led by a better principle than either
Reason or Counsel. We may, therefore, say in truth,
that the vocation of such persons of whom you
speak was indeed from God, but that the Lord
was satisfied with their firm intention of serving
Him in the religious state. God commanded Abraham to take Isaac, his beloved son, and to offer him
in sacrifice upon the mountain which He should
show him. However, at the moment when this holy
Patriarch stretched out his arm to strike his son,
an angel was dispatched to stop the father's arm,
and to assure him that God was satisfied with the
readiness of his obedience.

The man in the Gospel, whom Jesus Christ had
delivered from the devil, most humbly besought our
Lord to be allowed to stay with Him. Jesus Christ
was pleased with this desire, but did not wish it to
be accomplished; for the Gospel tells us, that our
Lord did not admit him, but said to him : "Go into
the house to thy friends, and tell them how great
things the Lord hath done for thee, and hath had
mercy on thee." (Mark v., 19.)

St. Francis Xavier wrote in a letter that he felt
inspired to go and preach the Gospel in China, and

that were he not to follow this inspiration, he might be lost. God was satisfied with his readiness to follow the inspiration, for He called the Saint out of this life before he could carry out his intention.

As God is satisfied with the readiness of certain persons to serve Him in the religious state, so they must acquiesce in the good pleasure of the Lord, if they cannot accomplish their design.

But as to yourself, it will be rather difficult for you to come to a better knowledge of God's will amidst the vanities and distractions of the world. Imitate, therefore, a certain young man, called Theodore, who, as we read in the life of St. Pachomius (C. 29), was an only son and heir to large possessions. On a certain festival he prepared a great banquet; on that occasion God made him understand that all riches would profit him nothing at the hour of death. So he went and shut himself up in his room, and besought the Lord, with many tears, to make known to him the state which he ought to choose in order to secure his eternal salvation. God inspired him to go into the monastery of Pachomius. He obeyed the inspiration; he forsook all things, and fled from his family. His mother went to St. Pachomius with an order from the emperor to restore her son; but Theodore prayed to God with so much fervor, that he obtained for his mother the grace to leave the world, and to retire into a convent. Imitate, I say, this example; retire a little from the noise of the world, in order to be able to raise your heart more than ordinarily above earthly things by means of prayer and meditation; purify your soul, if there is no reason to the contrary, by a general confession; read the little book which I will give you, and from which I have obtained so much lightand comfort concerning the marks of a religious vocation and the importance of following it; finally, present yourself before God in all humility and with a sincere desire of doing His will at the cost of any sacrifice. God gives "a good understanding to them that seriously wish to do well." Ask constantly of our Lord to give you light and strength to embrace that state, which will be more conducive to your salvation; that thus you may not afterwards, when your error shall be irreparable, have to repent for your whole life and for all eternity of the choice which you have made.

7*

CHAPTER VI.

WHEN a King levies soldiers to make war, his foresight and prudence require that he should prepare weapons to arm them. For what sense would there be in sending them to fight without arms ? If he did so, he would be taxed with great imprudence.

Now God acts in the same way. "He does not call," says St. Bernardine of Sienna, "without giving, at the same time, to those whom He calls, all that is required to accomplish the end for which He calls. So that when God calls a person to religion, He furnishes him with the physical, intellectual, and moral qualities necessary for the religious life. In other words, God not only gives him the *inclination*, but He also endows him with the *ability* for the performance of the duties annexed to that state of life.

As regards *ability*, the physical constitution of a person should be such as to aid, rather than prevent, the development of his intellectual and moral faculties; it should be sufficiently strong to endure the hardships of the religious life; and it should, moreover, be free from any hereditary disease. The mind of the postulant should be calm and deliberate; it should be strong, so as to be able to apply, if required, to study, or to many spiritual exercises, without danger of being deranged thereby. Weak minds will always be in danger of derangement from much mental application. This danger is so much the more to be apprehended if, at the same time, these persons are of a very nervous temperament, or of a rather scrupulous conscience, or if they are made to fast too much, or if they have led for a time a very sinful life; on account of which they will, in the ordinary course of Providence, sooner or later have to suffer many great temptations, which will bring upon them many hard mental afflictions and combats. Now all this weak minds cannot endure long, especially if guided—which may easily happen — by inexperienced or indiscret spiritual directors.

With regard to the intellectual faculties, a person need not have talents so brilliant as to make him a great mind; but he should have a sound, practical judgment, that is, common sense. ''Moins d'esprit, plus de jugement,'' as the French say. Neither great talents for some certain branches of science, nor piety and the spirit of devotion, can make up for a deficiency in judgment or common sense. Subjects of medium talents, yet gifted with a sound practical judgment, are generaly best suited for religious communities; because they are humble and docile. "Men of superior talents," says St. Vincent de Paul, "not possessing at the same time an unusual disposition to advance in virtue, are not good for us; for no solid virtue can take root in self-conceited and self-willed souls."

In reference to the intellectual faculties of a person, St. Francis de Sales expresses himself thus: "If I say that, in order to become a religious, one should have a good mind, I do not mean those great geniuses, who are generally vain and self-conceited, and in the world are but the receptacles of vanity. Such men do not embrace the religious life to humble themselves, but to govern others, and direct everything according to their own views and inclinations, as if the object of their entrance into religion was to be lecturers in philosophy and theology."

"When, therefore, I speak of a good mind, I mean well regulated and sensible minds, and also those of moderate powers, which are neither too great, nor too little; for such minds always do a great deal without knowing it; they set themselves to labor with a good intention, and give themselves to the practice of solid virtues. They are tractable, and allow themselves to be governed without much trouble ; for they easily understand how good a thing it is to let themselves be guided."

As to the moral. qualities of a person, they should be such as to suit a life in common. Hence he should easily agree with, and yield to others, and be of a cheerful, happy, gay, affable and sociable disposition. St. Francis de Sales says : "He should have a good heart, desiring to live in subjection and obedience." "If one sees the youthful aspirants to the religious institutes, here and abroad, in recreation or at study, he may easily decide who will persevere by a very simple rule. The joyous faces and the sparkling eyes denote the future monk far more surely than the demure looks and stolen glances." (Recollect. of Four last Popes, p. 39.)

There are many persons thus far qualified, but, for all that they are not called to religion, unless they experience, at the same time, an *inclination* for the religious life. Now this *inclination* is rothing else than the firm and constant will to serve God, in the *manner* and in the *place* to which His Divine Majesty calls one. In many, the will is so inflamed with the love of the religious life, that they embrace it without any question about it, and with exceedingly great pleasure. In others, and perhaps in the greater part of those who are called to

religion, this love or *inclination* for the religious
state is not so strong, but their understanding is so
much enlightened by the grace of God, that they dis-
cover the vanity and dangers of this world, seeing
also clearly, at the same time, the quiet, the safety,
the happiness, in a word, the inestimable treasures
of the religious life, though perhaps, as I have just
said, somewhat dull in their affection, and not so
ready to follow that which reason shows them. This
latter manner of *inclination*, or love for the religious
life, is better than the former, and is more generally
approved, by those who are experienced in these
matters, than the other, which consists only in a
fervent motion of the will ; for being grounded in
the light of reason and faith, it is less subject to
error, and more likely to last.

Now, in the opinion of St. Francis de Sales, *this
firm and constant will* of a person to serve God in
the *manner* and in the *place* where God calls him,
is the best mark of a good religious vocation. "But
observe," adds this enlightened Saint, "that when
I say a *firm and constant will* of serving God, I do
not say that a person should from the beginning
perform everything required by his vocation, and
that he should be perfect at once, and never feel
tempted, unsettled, and unshaken in his undertaking ; that he should never experience any doubts
as to his religious calling, or should not waver at

times, in a kind of irresolution, about his vocation : for this may happen from the weakness and re- pugnance of human nature, and the temptations of the devil, the arch enemy of all good. Oh no! that is not what I mean to say, for every one is more or less subject to passions, changes and vicissitudes; and a person will love one thing to-day and another thing to-morrow. No two days of our life are alike. To-day is different from yesterday, and to-morrow will be unlike either. It is not, then, by these dif- ferent movements and feelings that we ought to judge of the *firmness and constancy of the will*, but we should consider rather, whether amid this variety of movements, the will remains firm and unshaken, so as not to give up the good it has embraced ; so that to have a mark of a good vocation, we do *not* need a *sensible* constancy ; but a constancy which is in the *superior part of the soul*, and which is effective. Therefore, in order to know whether God calls us to religion, we must not wait for Him to speak to us sensibly, nor to send us an angel from heaven to make known to us His will ; still less do we need have revelations on this subject ; nor do we re- quire an examination by ten or twelve divines, to ascertain whether the inspiration be good or bad; whether we ought to follow it or not; "for advice and reflection are necessary," says St. Thomas Aquinas, "in *doubtful* affairs ; but not in that which regards religious vocation, which is *certainly good,* because it is recommended by our Lord Himself in the Gospel; the thought, therefore, of entering into religion needs no probation, but whosoever feels such an impulse in his soul, must admit of it, as of the voice of his Lord and Creator, and a voice which tends wholly to his own benefit; for we ought to correspond to it well, and cultivate the first movement of grace, and then not to distress ourselves if disgusts and coldness arise concerning it; for if we always strive to keep our will very firm in the determination of seeking the good which is shown to us, God will not fail to make all turn out well to His glory." Such a will is found in those young persons who, quietly and with consideration, prepare themselves for their retreat from the world, by trying to be given more to patience, prayer, penance, fasting, and the frequent reception of the sacraments. They are in earnest about the affair, and do not play, or if they do, it is at a good game, in which they can only be winners. They will not act as Lot's wife, who looked back, nor as the children of Israel, who longed for the flesh-pots of Egypt.

When the austerities and trials of a religious life have been fully represented to a person; when his admittance has been delayed, discouraged, nay, even refused for the sake of trial, and he still perseveres in his entreaties to be received into the Order, saying with St. Paul: "I can do all things in Him who strengthens me," such a person may also be considered to have such a good and firm will and a true vocation to the religious life.

One day a young man came to Don Bruno d'Affringues, requesting to be received into his Order. The venerable Superior seeing that he was of a delicate and weak constitution, represented to him the great severity of the Order. The young postulant replied, that he had previously taken that point into consideration, and that God would be his strength. The Superior, finding him so resolute, addressed him in a very sharp tone of voice, saying: "What are you thinking about, in wishing to enter our Order? Are you aware that every postulant, before he can be admitted, must perform a miracle? Can you perform it?" "Of myself I cannot," replied the young man, "but the power of God in me can. I have a firm confidence in His mercy, and hope that, having called me to His service in this Order, having instilled into my mind a great aversion for the world, He will certainly not permit me to return to the same, as I have sincerely forsaken it. Demand of me, venerable Father, what you please, God will accomplish it through me, as an evidence of my vocation." At these words, he appeared quite inflamed, and his whole countenance

6

was brightened. Don Bruno, astonished at such firmness, embraced the young man, and with tears in his eyes, he said to those present: ''Behold, my brethren, a vocation, that has undergone the Ordeal.'' He then turned to the young man and said: ''Have confidence, my son, God will ever assist and love you, and you will love and serve God, which is worth more than a miracle.''

When a person is wealthy, or has good prospects for temporal prosperity, yet wishes firmly to renounce everything in order to embrace a religious life, he must be considered to have a very good vocation.

Those who, in order to become religious, make great sacrifices, or suffer patiently unjust contradictions and ill-treatment from their friends, should be considered to have a true call.

When St. Columban was on the point of carrying out his resolution of entering into religion, his mother threw herself across the threshold to obstruct his passage; but he courageously stepped over her and hastened to the place of his vocation.

This good and firm will may also easily be supposed in those persons whose parents and ancestors are distinguished for their virtue and piety. The good fruit of the old tree before us, encourages us to hope, that the same kind of fruit will, in due time, follow the blossoms of the young tree : it being a law of nature, that a good tree brings forth good fruit.

"There are many persons," says St. Francis de Sales, "who feel the first inspirations to the religious life rather strongly; nothing appears difficult to them; they seem to be able to overcome all obstacles; but when they meet with these vicissitudes, and when these first feelings are not so sensible in the inferior part of their soul, they imagine that all is lost, and that they must give up every thing; they will, and they will not. What they then feel is not sufficient to make them leave the world. 'I should wish it,' one of these persons would say; 'but I do not know whether it is the will of God that I should be a religious, inasmuch as the inspiration which I now feel does not seem to me strong enough. It is quite true that I have felt it more strongly than I do at this moment; but as it is not lasting, I do not think that it is good.' Certainly when I meet with such souls, I am not astonished at this disgust and coolness; still less can I for that reason think that their vocation is not good. We must, in this case, take great pains to assist them and teach them, not to be surprised at these changes, but encourage them to remain firm in the midst of them. Well, I say to them, that is nothing; tell me, have you not felt in your heart the movement or inspiration to seek so great a good? 'Yes,'

they say, 'it is very true, but it passed away directly.' Yes, indeed, I answer, the force of the sentiment passed away, but not so entirely as not to leave
in you some affection of the religious life. 'Oh
no,' the person says; 'for I have always a sort of
feeling which makes me tender on that point; but
what troubles me is, that I do not feel this inclination so strongly as would be required for such a
resolution.' I answer them, that they must not be
troubled about these sensible feelings, nor examine
them too closely; that they must be satisfied with
that constancy of their will, which, amid all this,
does not lose the affection to its first design; that
they must only be careful to cultivate it well and to
correspond with this first inspiration. Do not care,
I say, from what quarter it comes, for God *has
many ways of calling His servants into His service*."

Although it be most desirable, and should be
held as a general rule, that a person should embrace
the religious life from the motive of securing better
his own salvation and sanctification, of working
more profitably for the salvation of others, and above
all, from the pure intention of serving God more
perfectly and of belonging to Him alone, yet it
cannot be denied that God does not draw all whom
He calls to His service by the same ways and means.

He sometimes makes use of preaching; sometimes of reading good books. Some are called

by hearing the sacred words of the Gospel, as St. Francis and St. Anthony were, by hearing these words: "Go, sell what thou hast, and give to the poor, and follow me," (Matt. 19, 21); and, "If any man come after Me, let him deny himself and take up his cross and follow Me." (Matt. 16, 24.)

Others have been called by the annoyances, disasters, and afflictions which came upon them in the world, which caused them to be disgusted with it, and to abandon it. There are but few who enter the service of God from the motive of belonging to and serving Him alone.

Among the women whose conversion is related in the Gospel, St. Magdalen was the only one who followed our Divine Saviour through love. The adultress came on account of her public disgrace; the woman of Canaan came that she might obtain relief in her temporal distress. St. Paul, the hermit, and Arsenius, withdrew into the desert to escape persecution. St Paul, the Simple, became a hermit on account of the unfaithfulness of his wife. Blessed Consalvus resolved to become a Dominican, because, while riding gaily and swiftly through the streets, he was thrown from his horse into a mud-puddle, and was laughed at by all those who were eye-witnesses. While yet in the mud-puddle, he said to himself: "Is it thus, treacherous world, that you treat me? You now deride me, but I also will

6*

laugh at you." This said, he abandoned the world and embraced the religious life.

Nicholas Bobadilla, a poor studen. of Paris, often went to see St. Ignatius Loyola, for the sake of relief in his temporal wants, but he soon felt attached to St. Ignatius, and became one of his first and most zealous companions.

The venerable Bernard of Corlione, in trying to escape the hands of human justice, fell into those of Divine mercy by joining the Capuchins.

Thomas Pounc, an Englishman, fell most awkwardly while dancing at a ball of the Queen of England. "Get up, you fool," said the Queen to him. The young man feeling highly offended, resolved to avenge himself on the world by quitting it. He entered the Society of Jesus, where he led a holy life; and after having suffered in a dungeon for twenty years, during the time of the religious persecution in England, he finished his life by sacrificing it, at last, for the sake of the faith.

"There are even others," says St. Francis de Sales,. "whose motives for embracing the religious life were still worse. I have heard, on good authority; that a gentleman of our age, distinguished in mind and person, and of good family, seeing some Capuchin Fathers pass by, said to the other noblemen who were with him, "I have a fancy to find out how these bare-footed men live, and to go amongst them, not meaning to remain there always, but only for three weeks or a month, so as to observe better what they do, and then mock and laugh at it afterwards with you." So he went and was received by the Fathers. But Divine Providence, who made use of these means to withdraw him from the world, converted his wicked purpose into a good one; and he who thought to take in others, was taken in himself; for no sooner had he lived a few days with those good religious, than he was entirely changed. He persevered faithfully in his vocation and became a great servant of God.

There are others, whose vocation is no better than this; those who go into religion on account of some natural defect, for instance, because they are lame, or blind of one eye, or ugly, or have some other similar defect; and what seems still worse is that they are sent into it by their parents, who very often, when they have a child that is half blind, lame, or otherwise defective, leave it by the fireside and say: "This one is good for nothing in the world; we must send him into religion; that will be so much burden taken off our hands," the children allowing themselves to be led as their parents wish. Thus many enter religion through disgust or weariness, or on account of disappointments or misfortunes. Such disappointments and troubles detach them from the love of creatures; they preserve

them from the delusion of false appearances, and
force them to enter into themselves; they purify
their hearts; they cause goodness to take root in
their souls; they give them a distaste for a life in
the world.   Would such souls have sought consolation only in God, if the world had loved them?
Would they have known the sweetness of God, if
the world had not maltreated and banished them
from its society?   It is God Who permits such
harsh treatment and refusals to befall them.   He
causes thorns to spring over all their pleasures, in,
order to prevent their reposing thereon.   They
would never have belonged to God, had the world
desired them; and they would have been adverse
to Him, had the world not been adverse to them.
It is thus that the Lord breaks the fetters by which
the world held them in bondge.

"There are souls," says St. Francis de Sales,
"who, were the world to smile upon them, would
never become religious, yet by means of contradictions and disappointments they are brought to despise the vanities and all allurements of the world,
and understand its fallacy."

"Our Lord has often made use of such means to
call many persons to His service whom He could
not have otherwise.   For though God is all-powerful and can do what He wills, yet He does not will
to take away the liberty which He has given us;

and when He calls us to His service, He will have us enter it willingly, and not by force or constraint. Now, though these persons come to God, as it were, in anger against the world, which has displeased them, or on account of some troubles and afflictions which have tormented them, yet they do not fail to give themselves to God of their own free will; and very often such persons succeed very well in the service of God, and become great Saints, sometimes greater than those who have entered it with more evident vocations or with far purer motives. God very often in these cases shows the greatness of His wisdom and divine goodness. He draws good from evil, by employing the intentions of these persons, which are by no means good in themselves, to make of those persons great servants of His Divine Majesty. Those whom the Gospel mentions as having been forced to partake of the feast did not, on that account, relish it less."

The Divine Artisan takes pleasure in making beautiful buildings with wood that is very crooked, and has no appearance of being fit for anything; and as a person who does not understand carpenter's work, seeing some crooked wood in his shop, would be astonished to hear him say it was meant for making some fine work of art (for he would say, how often must the plane pass over it before it can be fit for such a work?); so Divine Providence usually makes master-pieces out of these crooked and sinister intentions. He makes the lame and the blind come into His feast to show us that we need not have two eyes or two feet to enter Paradise ; that it is better to go to heaven with one leg, one eye, or one arm, than to have two and be lost. Now this class of persons having entered religion in this way, have often been known to make great progress in virtue and persevere faithfully in their vocation. It cannot be expected that all should commence with perfection. It matters little in what manner we begin, provided we are resolved to attain our end by strenuous efforts. As fowlers have not one kind of net, nor one kind of bait to catch fowls, but some for one kind, and some for another, so God bends and applies Himself to the several natures of men, both for their benefit, and to maintain the sweetness of His fatherly Providence over all. He called Peter and Andrew from their boats, and Matthew from the Custom House, because the one was a publican, and the others fishermen ; He took Paul in the heat of his zeal of persecuting the church, because that was then his *determination;* so in all religious vocations, one is called upon one occasion, and another upon another, and some out of the midst of their sins. We must then revere and esteem the incomprehensible ways and inscrutable judgments of God in this great variety of the vocations and means which He makes use or to draw His creatures to His service; with St. Paul we must exclaim: *"O the height of the riches of the wisdom and knowledge of God! How incomprehensible are His judgments and how unsearchable His ways!"*

Now from this great multiplicity of vocations and variety of motives it follows that it is often a difficult matter to form a correct judgment, as to whether a person is called to a religious life. This difficulty, however, vanishes in a great measure, if we apply the mark above given, viz, that among the several marks of a good vocation the best and surest of them all is, *the firm and constant will to serve God* in *the manner* and *in the place* to which one feels called by His Divine Majesty.

The *inclination*, then, for the religious life im_plies not only the firm and constant will to serve God in religion in general, but it implies also the particular attraction to a life either exclusively contemplative or active, or mixed. This attraction must be well inquired into, as it cannot be expected that a man will faithfully persevere in a manner of life for which he feels no particular liking: it being almost impossible for human nature to go, for a life time, against a torrent.

Although *Ability* and *Inclination*, taken in the sense just explained, generally suffice to prove the religious vocation of a person, yet there are better and more evident marks than these, viz :

1. *Divine revelation.* St. Paul the Apostle, St. Alóysius de Gonzaga, St. Stanislas, and other Saints, are examples of this kind.

2. *Special inspirations*, by which a person is suddenly enlightened, and vehemently urged on to a life of perfection, and sweetly forced, as it were, thereto.

But is it not true, a soul may say, that the devil has often transformed himself into an angel of light and has deceived many a pious soul. I fear, that the desire which I now experience to be a religious, may perhaps come from Satan, in order to bring me to greater destruction, foreseeing, perhaps, as he may, that I will not persevere.

I answer, you have no reason to fear this; for what has the devil to do with perpetual chastity, with obedience, with the voluntary humiliation of ourselves, being, as he is, the prince of pride and hating, as he does, nothing more than these virtues? And if this wicked spirit cannot move us to any particular virtue, as to the love of God, to a greater faith, or hope in Him, or to true and solid humility, no more than ice can be the cause of fire, or fire of ice, much less can he move us to that virtue which, in a manner, comprehends all virtues.

But could it even be supposed for a moment that he could inspire such a desire, there would be no danger, says St. Thomas Aquinas. For as long as he suggests that which is common for good angels to put into our mind, there is nothing to be feared, because we are not forbidden to benefit ourselves by our enemy, especially when we know not that it is our enemy. Moreover, though the devil should move us to embrace the religious life, he could never move us so effectually, unless God did inwardly draw us. *The devil will not divide his own kingdom;* which he really would do, were he to go about and thrust sin out of a man's soul, or, which is the same thing, bring a man to a place where he may easily rid himself of it. Nor is he such a fool, or so little skilled in his warfare against souls, as to let go the prey which he holds in his claws, and suffer it to save itself in so strong a hold and a place which so much annoys him, and he himself to help him forward to that place, with the hope that he shall recover him afterwards with greater gain. Do then no longer mind such a foolish fear, but rest assured, that your holy desire for the religious life is from God, Who in this manner manifests His voice and calls you to come and receive from Him, for your attire, the richest robe—the grace of vocation to the religious life.

CHAPTER VII.

THE Church is a body, of which Jesus Christ is the head, and all the faithful are members. Each one is gifted with different functions, though all are animated by the same spirit. The good and perfection of a member consists in remaining contentedly in the place which God has assigned him, and in performing well the duties of its state. If the hand wishes to be in the place of the eye, and the eye wishes to be where the hand is, these two become burdensome, and disturb the good order and harmony of the body ; and being through perversity without nourishment, because they are engaged in an unnatural war, they become lifeless, and are a scandal to the other members and an offence to their head. This is the comparison which is made use of by St. Paul.

It is the same with all men. God has assigned to each one a place and function in His Church, and to each state He has attached peculiar blessings for those who are faithful. If we are in the state, or engaged in the employment or occupation which God has chosen for us, we enjoy a profound peace ; we rest under His protection ; we are nourished by His grace; we are enriched by His blessings ; and work out our salvation with but little pain, and infallibly arrive at perfection.

The subject of vocation, however, is considered by most persons in the world as one of trifling importance ; it seems to them to be indifferent whether we live in the state to which God has called us, or in that which we have chosen for ourselves, according to our own fancy ; hence so many lead disorderly lives and are lost. Now it is certain, on the contrary, that our eternal salvation principally depends on our choice of a state of life. Upon vocation follows justification, upon justification follows glorification, which is eternal life ; and he who deranges this order, and breaks this chaim of salvation, will fail to save his soul, whatever efforts he may make, or whatever labors he may undergo ; and it is to such that St. Augustine says, "You run well, but you are out of the road." You are out of the path by which God called you to walk to obtain your salvation.

The Lord does not accept the sacrifices which we offer Him according to our own will. He had no regard for Cain and his gifts. And He threatens those with the heaviest chastisements who despise His call and follow the counsels of their own hearts instead of following His direction. "Woe to you, apostate children," said He by the mouth of His prophet, "that you would take counsel, and not of Me; and would begin a web, and not by My spirit."

The divine vocation to a perfect life is an especial and very precious grace which God does not bestow upon all; and, therefore, He has reason to be displeased with those who despise it. How much would a prince be offended if, having called one of his vassals to his service in preference to a courtier or favorite, this vassal should refuse to obey him? And shall not God resent a similar insult? Ah! He does indeed resent such an injury, and thus He threatens, "Woe to him that gainsayeth his Maker:" the word *woe* signifies, in the language of Scripture, eternal perdition. The chastisement of the disobedient man begins even in this life, in which he never finds rest. "Who hath resisted Him," says holy Job, "and hath lived in peace?" and therefore he fails to receive such special and efficacious graces as God bestows upon His beloved children, and which are so necessary in order to persevere in the practice of virtue and to attain eternal life. Hence, as the theologian Habert says, he will with great difficulty save his soul. With great difficulty will he work out his salvation ; and like a limb out of joint, he can scarcely live a regular life. Although, strictly speaking, he may be enabled to save his soul, yet it will be with great difficulty that he will enter upon the right way and work out his eternal salvation. St. Bernard calls the ingratitude of not following the vocation of God ''a scorching wind, drying up the fountain of piety, the dew of mercy, and the stream of grace.''

St. Gregory, writing to the Emperor Maurice, who, by an edict, had forbidden his soldiers to become religious, said that it was an unjust law which closed the gates of Paradise to many, because there are many who cannot be saved unless they leave all things and embrace the religious state.

A remarkable case is related by Father Lancizio of a youth of great talent in the Roman College, who, whilst making a retreat, asked his confessor if it was a sin not to correspond to a vocation to the religious life. The confessor replied that it was not in itself a grievous sin, for such a vocation was rather a counsel than a command, but that it would greatly endanger his eternal salvation. The young man, however, did not obey the call. He went afterwards to pursue his studies at Macerata, where he soon began to neglect the exercise of prayer and of holy communion, and at length gave himself up

7*

to a wicked life ; and soon after, as he was one
night leaving a house of ill-fame, he was mortally
wounded by a rival.   A priest ran to his assistance,
but the young man expired before the minister of
God reached him.   Thus did God make known the
chastisement which is prepared for those who despise
their vocation.

At Turin, a young man gifted with fine qualities
had resolved to leave the world, but he was turned
from his resolution by a friend, or rather by an
enemy, whose affectionate letters painted the world
to his imagination in such ravishing colors that he
gave up the thought of entering the house of God.
The spiritual Father of this deluded young man
heard of the perfidy of his friend, and wrote to him
to cease his diabolical attempts, and if he desired the
salvation of his companion, to advise him to fulfil
his good resolution.   "If you do not," said he,
"you will experience what recently happened to a
young man who left the service of God by the persuasion of another.   He lived an abandoned life,
was implicated in a robbery, and died on the gal-
lows."   All this was useless; the seducer persisted
and the young man obeyed him.   After some days
he was arrested with a band of robbers that had
just assassinated some travelers. From his dungeon he wrote to the Priest that his threat had
been a prophecy, for he was then in irons as an

assassin. To the great dishonor of his family, he was at once condemned to death. Thus the word of the wise man was fulfilled: "Because they have not consented to My counsel, but despised all My reproof, therefore they shall eat the fruit of their own way, and shall be filled with their own devices." (Prov. 1, 30, 31.)

A very destinguished lady received many favors from God, as long as she remained at home, passing her time in exercises of piety : and as the grace of vocation was among these favors, she resolved to consecrate her virginity to God. But by degrees she left her retreat, gave herself more liberty, and finally became very fond of a young gentleman, who, in his turn, conceived an affection for her. She forgot her vocation, and thought only of hastening her marriage. To celebrate the day with great pomp, a numerous train followed her to the house of her betrothed. But in descending from her carriage she slipped, fell and broke her neck. Thus, she expired before the door of the house which her own will had chosen, instead of the cloister to which God called her.

When the Countess Blanche retired to a monastery, it was feared that she would abandon it on account of the four enemies which beset her : these were her noble birth, her remarkable beauty, her youth, and the remembrance of her riches. Cardinal Peter Damian wrote to the Countess, and, to encourage her to persevere, related the tragical history of a great princess who had disregarded her vocation. It is as follows: Dominica, of Gielva, a princess of dazzling beauty, married a Doge of Venice, and passed her life in pleasure and luxury, without troubling herself with the service of God. The purest dews of Heaven were collected for her baths; to save her trouble, her food was nicely minced at table by her servants, and her chamber was filled with the most precious perfumes. You can form no idea of the luxury that surrounded her. Every day she spent several hours before her mirror in painting herself, and would not allow a single hair to be out of place. Divine Justice did not fail to overtake her. In a horrible sickness her flesh putrefied, and the stench which came from her sores was so insupportable that she resembled carrion devoured by worms. Her maids and servants fled from her. A single attendant ventured from time to time to carry her some food in a silver bowl, but provided herself with perfumes, and retired quickly to avoid fainting. What a sight! to see this princess— lately so nicely perfumed, now nothing but corruption! the body that wore such costly attire, now nothing but ulcers! her who received the homage of all the great, now left to her servants! She, to whose pleasure nature and art could not contribute enough, now lay eaten up by cancers, plunged in filth, a burden to herself, and insupportable to others. A little while ago she would not allow one to speak to her of death; now, death is the object of her most ardent desires. How terrible is the sentence passed by God infinitely just: "I called and you refused; you have despised My councel and neglected My reprehensions. I also will laugh in your destruction, and will mock when that shall come to you which you feared. When sudden calamity shall fall upon you, you shall call upon Me, and I will not hear because you have not con_ sented to My counsel." (Prov. 1: 24–30.)

Another instance is related by Father Pinamonti. A certain novice was thinking of abandoning the religious life. Jesus Christ Himself appeared to him, seated on His throne, and commanded, with great severity, that his name should be erased from the book of life, which so terrified him that he persevered in his vocation.

How many such examples do we read in the annals of history! How many miserable young people shall we see condemned on the day of judgment for not having obeyed their vocation

For those who have rebelled against the light of the Holy Ghost, it seems a just punishment that they should be deprived of the light; and for those who have refused to walk in the way assigned to them by the Lord, preferring one which they have chosen for themselves without light, that they should be lost. "Because you have despised My calling," says the Lord, "I also will laugh in your destruction, and will mock when that shall come to you which you feared." That is to say, God will not listen to the cry of those who despise His voice. St. Augustine says, "Those who have despised the voice of God when it invited them, shall feel the vengeance of His justice for their contempt."

When, therefore, God calls us to the state of perfection, if we would not endanger our eternal salvation, we must obey, and obey instantly, unless prevented by a very grievous reason.

When the devil sees that he cannot succeed in making one give up the resolution of entering into Religion, he suggests various causes of delay. To some he suggests their youth; to others that they must take longer time to consider, consult with their friends, have a good trial of their strength and some experience by the practice of good works before hand, in order thus to prepare for more difficult matters.

Now there is one excellent answer to all these temptations, that is, to persuade ourselves and to acknowlege as a certain truth that any kind of delay in so profitable and wholesome a matter is not only to no purpose, but is exceedingly dangerous.

For this reason all holy men, knowing how many wicked snares lie hidden under these deceitful deliberations, cry to us with one voice to break off all delays and procrastinations in this matter. "Make haste," writes St. Jerome, "I beseech you, and seeing your ship stuck in the sands, cut the rope asunder rather than untie it." This Saint here means to say, that as in a vessel on the point of sinking, a man would rather think to cut the ropes than untie them, so should a man who is in the midst of the world seek to fly from it as soon as possible, that he may escape from the danger of eternal perdition, which is there so easy.

St. John Chrysostom, in one of his Homilies to the people on the beauty and pleasure of the religious life, concludes thus: "Perhaps many of you are now warm at heart, and burn with a great desire of so beautiful a state of life. But what will it benefit you, if while you are here you have this fire, and as soon as you go out you quench it, and the flame and heat disappear? What remedy? While your love is yet hot, go presently to those angels, and there enkindle it more. Do not say, I will first speak with my friends; I will dispatch my business. This delay is a beginning of shrinking away. The devil is at hand eager to insinuate himself into your mind, and if he can bring about but a short delay, he will succeed in bringing you to great coldness; therefore, it is said, '*Delay not from day to day.*'"

"Behold," says St. Augustine, "the Giver of mercy opens the gate to you. Why do you delay entering? You should be glad, if He should open to you at any time upon your knocking. You did not knock, and yet He opened; and do you dare remain still without? O, do not delay. The Holy Scripture says of the works of mercy: *Do not say, go and come again; to-morrow, I will give*, when you can presently do well; for you know not what may happen the day following. You have heard the commandment of not deferring to be merciful towards another, and are you cruel towards yourself by delays? Give alms to your own soul. I do not say you should give it anything, but do not put aside the hands of *Him* Who gives."

But why quote the opinions of the Fathers of the Church on this subject? Have we not the authority of the Gospel for it, in the prompt obedience of the Apostles? Have we not a strong confirmation of its necessity when we read that the Diciple wished to bury first his father, and Christ would not led him—but answered: "Follow Me, leave the dead to bury their dead;" and to another who asked only to bid those at home farewell, the Divine Wisdom said: "No man putting his hand to the plough and looking back is apt for the Kingdom of heaven."

What is the drift of the pretence of taking advice, or making some trial of ourselves, but a cloak to hide the snares which the devil lays for us, and the secret love of the world, which we do not like openly to acknowledge, in order that thus we may be longer in leaving what we leave unwillingly? This is indeed most dangerous; for nothing is easier than never to forsake that with which we so unwillingly part.   These lights, inspirations and movements of God are transient, not permanent, and therefore, as St. Thomas Aquinas says, the divine call to a perfect life should be followed *instantly.*

St. Antoninus relates the sad history of a young man of rare talents, who was called by God to the Order of St. Francis, and who resolved to enter it, but deferred his entrance from day to day.   To increase the delay, he accepted the care of a parish. After a few days he was seized with a violent fever, and, that the world might know the cause of this punishment, he exclaimed in a frightful tone: "Ah! unhappy me; I have despised the voice of God: Alas! I am lost."   They begged him to make his confession, but he refused, saying: "I am damned." They at first thought he was out of his senses, but in the end saw that he was perfectly sensible.   They spoke of the mercy of God, and urged him to promise obedience to his vocation, to kiss the crucifix and make a good confession.   He replied: "I will not, confess.   I have seen Almighty God in wrath against

8

me. I have heard from His mouth this irrevocable sentence: 'I have called thee, thou hast refused Me: therefore, depart into hell.'" After these words, the young man expired. Are you astonished at this? It is not at all strange, for St. Anselm says: "How many have I known to promise and delay, who have been so surprised by death, that they have neither been able to enjoy what induced them to delay, nor fulfil what they had promised!"

If it is so very important to follow our vocation promptly, it is not less important to persevere in it. The evil spirit always envies our perseverance in the good which we have commenced, because he knows this to be the only good that shall be rewarded. It is not enough to commence well, we must also finish well. "He who perseveres to the end shall be saved." No man is paid for unfinished articles. We must then finish the good which we have commenced. The Holy Ghost admonishes every one thus: "Let every man abide in the calling in which he was called." (I. Cor. 7 : 20,) for, "Blessed is the man that shall continue in wisdom—and that considereth her ways in his heart." (Eccles. 14 : 22, 23.) "Blessed that religious," observes Cornelius a Lapide on this passage, "who well considers his vocation and institute, penetrates into and admires its wisdom, and endeavors, with all his strength and heart, to comply with all its precepts and duties."

God permits the devil to try the faithfulness and
constancy of His servants in their holy vocation.
One of the most usual temptations which our enemy
makes use of to shake our constancy is, to excite in
us disgust and dissatisfaction for our manner of life.
Hence it is, says St. Francis de Sales, that we so
often hear people complain of their state of life. It
is one of the usual temptations of the enemy to make
us feel discontented and to render us unhappy.
Whilst we are so often admonished by the Holy
Ghost to be satisfied with the condition in which we
are placed, the evil spirit continually incites us to
wish for a change. It is a great secret and great
perfection to remain firm in the boat of life in which
God has quartered us. We fancy that by changing
our ship we shall fare better : yes, if we changed
ourselves. My God, I am a sworn enemy of these
useless, dangerous and bad desires. God wills to
speak to us amidst the thorns and the bush (Exod.
3: 2), and we will Him to speak to us in *"the
whistling of a gentle air."* (3 Kings 19: 12.) We
ought then to remain on board the ship in which
we are, in order to cross from this life to the other;
and we ought to remain there willingly and with
affection, because, although we should not have
been placed there by the hand of God, but by the
hand of man, still, once there, God wills us to be
there, and consequently we ought to be there sweetly and willingly.

"Let us, therefore, not think of anything else; let us not sow our wishes in other people's gardens; let us not wish for that which we are not, but let us earnestly desire to be the very best of what we are. Let us endeavor to do our best to perfect ourselves where we are, and bear manfully all the crosses, light or heavy, that we may encounter. *Believe me, this is the leading principle, and yet the one least understood in the spiritual life.* Every one follows his own taste; very few place their happiness in fulfilling their duty according to the pleasure of our Lord. Where is the use of building castles in Spain when we are ordered to live in France. 'As a bird that wandereth from her nest, so is a man that leaveth his place,' (Prov. 27: 8,) [his studies, his charge, his occupation, his spiritual exercises, or station of life, etc.] Let every one remain firm in his vocation, if he wishes to ensure his tranquillity of mind, peace of heart, progress in virtue and holiness of life."

To become unfaithful to our vocation is for us to suffer as many pangs as a limb which, through some accident, has been wrenched out of place. We are continually tormented by evil spirits, who have power over a soul that is out of its proper sphere of action. We are no longer under the protection of God, since we have withdrawn from His guidance, and voluntarily left His watchful Providence. We fall often and grievously, because we are unsustained by the grace which belongs to the state in which God desires us to be. Thus we lose our devotion, neglect our prayers, and give ourselves no trouble to seek God; and if we do seek Him, we find an angry God, who reproaches us incessantly with our infidelity, and with the contempt we have shown His service. We hear a voice, which admonishes us day and night, from the depths of our souls: You are not where God designed you to be. You are not doing that which He ordered you to do. It is not He who sent you to this place. It is not He who has given you this commission. Instead of a recompense, you shall receive from Him severe chastisements.

St. Ephrem, the Syrian, writes: "You must love to stay in that place which God has assigned to you; there you must fly idleness and laziness; for it is not by changing our place of abode that our passions will be crushed, but only by constant watchfulness over them. And St. Bernard, in his thirty-second letter to the Abbot St. Nicasius, writes thus: "Tell brother Hugo, on my part, not to believe every spirit, and not to give up so soon what is certain for what is uncertain, remembering that the devil envies us nothing so much as our perseverance, which he tries to shake to the utmost of his power; for he knows but too well that this virtue alone

8*

will be crowned; let him understand that it is safer for him simply to persevere in his present vocation, than to give it up under the specious pretext of obtaining a greater good. "Withdraw yourself from such a temptation," writes St. Francis de Sales to a religious; "treat it as you would treat that of blasphemy, of treason, of heresy, of despair. Do not discourse with it; do not capitulate; do not listen to it; cross it as much as you can by frequent renewal of your vows, by frequent submissions to your superiors." "I feel an extreme compassion," wrote St. Alphonsus to his brethren in religion, "when I think of those who were once our brethren in religion and who lived in peace, and under obedience, united to God, and contented with everything that happened to them: and now they are in the midst of the world, in confusion and disturbance. They have indeed the liberty to go where they like, but do what they may, all is without regularity, without interior spirit, and without quiet. From time to time they will think of making meditation, but when their infidelity to God, and their ingratitude to Him in having abandoned their vocation, stares them in the face, the remorse of conscience which they feel is too acute; and hence it comes to pass that, in order to avoid the bitterness of that remorse, they often give up prayer; and so their lukewarmness and their disquiet of mind increases more and more.

"Their misfortune did not begin with grievous faults, but with little defects; and the devil made use of these to bring them little by little to the loss of their vocation. I repeat, I pity them from the bottom of my heart; for I am certain that their whole life is nothing but confusion and disquiet; and if their life is full of straits, much more so will be their death. Some years ago I had hard work to comfort one of these, who at the thought of the loss of his vocation became insane, and cried out in a frenzy that he was damned, and that there was no salvation for him, because he had voluntarily lost his vocation."

History is full of such fatal instances. F. Jerome Piatti tells us of a novice who was visited by a relation, who said to him, "Listen to me; I only speak because I love you, and I beg you to reflect that your constitution is not fitted to undergo the fatigues and labors of the religious life; by remaining in the world you may please God better, and bestow on the poor the riches with which He has blessed you. If you persist in your undertaking you will repent of it, for after a little time you will be obliged to quit the community in disgrace, or you will be only able to perform the offices of cook or porter, on account of your want of talents and indifferent health; it is therefore wiser to do at once what you will be obliged to do at last." The poor young man, thus urged, left the monastery, and many days had not elapsed before he fell into all kinds of vices; and in a quarrel with some rivals, he, together with the relative who had perverted him, was so severely wounded that they both died on the same day; and what is still worse, the unfortunate novice expired without confession, of which he must have stood in so great need.

It is related by Father Casalicchio, that a certain knight, when on the point of entering the house of a woman of ill-fame one night, heard the bell of the Capuchin monastery toll for the office, upon which he cried out, "O, how can I dare to offend God at the very moment in which His servants are about to praise Him?" And having been thus called by the Lord, he afterward entered that Order. But his mother did and said everything in her power to make him return to her, and at last succeeded. And what was the consequence? Only a few months afterwards the young man was slain by some enemies, and his dead body carried on a board to his mother.

Denis, the Carthusian, relates that two novices of his Order, having been perverted by their parents, left the convent. Not many days after their departure the father of the two youths, as well as themselves, died of the plague; and, sad to relate, as the author remarks, they had a bad death.

F. Mancinelli informs us that a young man of

noble birth, though he had entered religion and had resisted with great courage all the arts of his mother, who left nothing untried to divert him from his purpose, at length yielded to her entreaties and continnal pursuit, and unhappily left the community. The mother, having accomplished her desire, sought to procure him all sorts of wordly amusements, and made him take lessons in fencing. But, alas! for one day as the youth was engaged in that exercise with a friend, he received a blow on the eye, from the violence of which he died upon the spot, and without confession.

Father Casalicchio writes, that when he was giving a mission in a place near Cosenza, called Caroli, he heard of a young man who was withdrawn from the Capuchin monastery; first his father went and demanded, with great boldness, so as to cause a great disturbance in the monastery, that his son should be given back to him; afterwards he sent one of his brothers, with several armed companions, among whom there was a brother-in-law of the young man, and they effected his removal by force. Attend to the sequel. A month afterwards the father lost his life in a tempest which overtook him in a voyage at sea. At the end of sixty days the brother-in-law died at a distance from his home, and the body of the unhappy novice, who had been unfaithful to his vocation, was within a short space of time covered with sores, so that from head to food he became an entire wound, and soon died in a fit of convulsions; and God only knows in what disposition of soul he died.

We read also in the life of St. Camillus de Lellis, that a young man who had entered his community at Naples was greatly persecuted by his father. The good novice at first withstood him very courageously; but having occasion to go to Rome he had an interview with his father again, and this time yielded to the temptation. On dismissing him the saint predicted to him that he would come to an evil end and die by the hand of justice, which was verified, for the young man, who had married, at length, in a fit of jealousy, murdered his wife and two servants; and having been apprehended by justice, notwithstanding that his father-expended his whole fortune to save the life of his unhappy son, he was publicly beheaded at Naples, nine years after his departure from the monastery. It is related also, in the life of the same Saint, that to another novice who desired to return to the world, St Camillus announced the chastisements of God; he, however, left the convent and went to Messina, where, six months afterwards, he died suddenly without the sacraments.

The misfortune of these miserable souls should make us be determined to suffer everything rather than the loss of vocation.

"Stand firm, therefore," says the Holy Ghost, "in the lot set before thee, and in prayer to the most high God," that is, be firm and constant in repelling all suggestions and temptations of the world, the flesh and the devil, inducing you to give up your vocation. Be likewise assiduous in prayer to God and the Blessed Virgin for strength and courage to be able to lead a life worthy of and corresponding to your vocation. As soon as you have been called to a certain state of life, cast your anchors well, in order that your vessel may not, by degrees, be driven off on the wide ocean, and experience will soon teach you what calm and peace you will enjoy in the harbor." (St. Ephrem, Adhortat. 4.) "For the life of a laborer that is content with what he hath shall be sweet, and in it thou shalt find a treasure." (Eccles. 40: 18.) The religious state is "a tree of life to them that lay hold on it; and he that shall retain it is blessed." (Prov. 3: 18.)

"O let us never cease," wrote St. Alphonsus to his brethren in religion, "to thank God, and let us pray Him to aid us in valuing this great gift aright, this gift which has not been granted to so many others, who are our countrymen and our friends. What claims had we more than they? Perhaps only our greater iniquities; and yet God, notwithstanding our unworthiness, has delivered us out of this miserable world. I am not alarmed by the fear of poverty, or of sickness, or of persecutions: the only fear that terrifies me is lest any one of you should one day be seduced by some passion to leave the house of God, and should go into the midst of the world, as has happened to so many who were once in the congregation, and who now are out of it, and live without peace. And even if some of these should save their souls, they nevertheless will find that they have lost that beautiful crown which God had prepared for them in heaven, if they had persevered in their vocation.

"Therefore, my dearest brothers, let us always pray to Jesus Christ, and to our Mother Mary, that God of His mercy may grant to us all the gift of perseverance."

CHAPTER VIII.

THE story of Flavia Domitilla's life is very interesting. She was a person of high rank, being cousin to the Emperors Titus and Domitian, and what was much better, many of her relations were saints and martyrs; for she was the daughter of St. Plautilla, and niece to Flavius Clemens, who also was a martyr. She had two servants, Nereus and Achilleus, who were brothers, and had been converted by the preaching of St. Peter. They were so much more faithful and well conducted than any of her other servants; that she could not help noticing them; and when she came to speak to them, she was even more pleased with them. They said that they were Christians; and when she asked them what it was to be a Christian, they told her all about a future state, and the great day of judgment, and Jesus Christ having become man, and having died on a cross to save sinners. She liked very much to hear them speak about these things, and she used very often to escape from her gay companions, and go to talk quietly with them, till at last she was converted, and was baptized.

As Flavia Domitilla was of the Emperor's family, and was besides very rich, many young noblemen wished to marry her; and after some time her friends engaged her to Aurelian, a handsome and agreeable young man of high birth. Domitilla was very much pleased with the idea of this marriage, and being a gay young girl, she thought only of dressing herself and making herself look as beautiful as she could, in order that Aurelian might be the more in love with her. One day when she was busy choosing the most elegant dress she could think of, and arranging all her jewels, so as to be most becoming to her, her two faithful servants, Nereus and Achilleus, said to her, "Ah! dear Madam, if you would but take the same care to adorn your soul with virtues, as you do to deck out your body, you would not fail to win the love of Jesus Christ, the King of heaven; and He would take you to be His spouse, and then this beauty of yours, which will now so quickly fade, would last forever, and you would become even much more beautiful than you are now, and would shine gloriously in the Court of Heaven." Domitilla did not much fancy this sort

of advice, and she answered : "All that is very true ;
but still there is no sin in marrying ; and if I am to
marry, I may just as well take pains to set myself
off properly, and to win the love of my husband, so
that I may be happy in my marriage." Then Nereus
replied : "You look only on the pleasures of this
life, which so quickly pass away, and do not think
about the everlasting happiness of heaven; you
look on the advantages of marriage, and not on the
trouble and misery which it may bring on you."
And then he and Achilleus went on to show her
how, when she became a wife, she gave herself up
to a man of whom she could know but little till she
went to live with him, and who would, perhaps, treat
her very unkindly.   For if he took a fancy, he
might shut her up and not let her see her father and
mother or any of her old friends; or if he were
jealous, he might be angry with her for every word
she spoke, and everything she did innocently ; or if
he were ill-tempered, he might beat her, and use
rough and harsh language to her.   And then, if she
should have children, they would be a continual
cause of anxiety and trouble to her, from the very
time of their birth, for they would be ill, or they
would be hurting themselves, or they would be disobedient and unruly, or they would not be so clever
or so handsome as she wished them to be ; and then
there would be the care of nursing them, and teach-

ing them, and putting them forward in the world; and perhaps, after all, they would die young, or what is worse, they might live to be a disgrace to their family, and a curse both to themselves and to their parents. They said all this and much more, which might well make a young girl think twice before she married.

After they had gone through all the troubles and anxieties of marriage, Nereus began to speak of the blessed state of virginity. "A virgin," said he, "lives on earth the life which the angels live in heaven, and she will have in heaven a bright crown which is given to no one but virgins. She has God for her husband, and she knows that He can never treat her unkindly; whatever she tries to do for love of Him, He will be pleased with; He will never neglect her or forsake her, but He will always be with her, speaking sweetly to her, and putting happy and holy thoughts into her heart; and she will be free from all the cares of this world, and will not be afraid of sickness or any misfortunes that may happen to her, for His arms will always be round her, His beautiful countenance will always be smiling on her, and the thought of His love will be a paradise of unspeakable happiness to her. Think, then, my dear young mistress, which husband is the best, and choose him whom you think you can love most—either a mortal man, who, be

he ever so good, will one day die and leave you, or
Jesus Christ, Who will never die, but Who will
rejoice and bless you with His company for ever
and ever."

Domitilla was very much struck with what Nereus
and Achilleus said. Her conscience told her that
they were right, and a voice within her seemed to
call her to be the spouse of Jesus. But how could
she give up all the things of which she was so fond?
Her beautiful dresses, her costly jewels, the gay
company she was in the habit of keeping, and, above
all, the love of Aurelian? It was a hard struggle
between the love of God and the love of the world;
and for a short time it seemed as if the world must
conquer. For the devil whispered to her that, after
all, there was no need to give up all these things,
for why could not she marry Aurelian, and yet love
Jesus, as many married women did. But then there
flashed across her mind the words of the Apostle
St. Paul, "The virgin thinketh on the things of the
Lord, that she may be holy both in body and in
spirit. But she that is married thinketh on the
things of the world, how she may please her husband." And she felt and knew that it was her
whole self our Lord was asking of her, and that He
would not be satisfied if she gave Him only half her
heart. So she tried to look at the matter simply
and earnestly, and she prayed to God to guide her

7*

and to give her strength to do His will, whatever it might be. At last the grace of God triumphed, and she exclaimed, "Would to God I had heard all this before I was engaged to be married. But, even now, it may not be too late, and God may yet open to me some means by which I may get free from Aurelian." On hearing these words, Nereus and Achilleus gave fervent thanks to God, Who, by His grace, had brought their mistress into such a good disposition of mind; and they earnestly exhorted her to make an offering of herself to God, and to trust confidently and lovingly in Him. The next question was how she was to break off her marriage. This was a subject which required some considera-tion; for it was not to be supposed that Aurelian would submit quietly to lose his rich and beautiful young wife; and if he made any disturbance about it, her change of religion would come to the ears of the emperor, who was beginning just then to perse-cute the Christians. And now the devil set before her the trials that she was going to draw on herself —the dark dungeon, the scourging, the rack, the wild beasts, the fire, and all the horrible torments that were inflicted on Christians; and he asked her how a thoughtless young girl like herself, who had spent her life in dressing and amusing herself, could bear such things as these. All that he put into her head seemed very sensible, and when she thought about the tortures she could not help shuddering, and she felt that if she thought much about these things she should not have the courage to keep to her resolution. So she determined to put away all these thoughts with which the devil was tempting her, and not to trouble herself about consequences; and she committed herself gently to the care of her dearest spouse, Jesus, trusting entirely to His love, and beseeching Him to take care of her and to give her strength to do His will and to bear whatever trials He might send her

Nereus and Achilleus, meanwhile, had gone to the Pope, St. Clement, and had told him that she wished to consecrate her virginity to Jesus, and to become His spouse instead of marrying Aurelian. The Church of Rome was now in great trouble on account of the persecution, and the Holy Father was in constant anxiety for those of his flock who were being persecuted, lest they should not bear their trials with fortitude. It was, therefore, a great joy and encouragement to him that a young girl like Flavia Domitilla should wish, in a time like this, to consecrate herself to God's service, for he knew that nothing but the grace of God could lead her to make such a holy resolution. He was filled with joy and courage, and he exclaimed:—
"It seems to me that the time is not far off, when our Lord will be pleased to crown you, and me, and

Domitilla with martyrdom ; and since He commands us not to fear those who kill the body, but cannot hurt the soul, let us not care for the displeasure of the emperor, but let us boldly obey God, Who is the Sovereign Lord of heaven and earth." He then went with Nereus and Achilleus to the house of Flavia Domitilla, and after talking to her, and finding that she had a true vocation, and was ready to suffer everything for the love of Jesus, he consecrated her to be His spouse and to spend her life in loving and serving Him.

It was not long before the troubles which Domitilla expected came upon her. At first, Aurelian would not believe that she really meant to break off the marriage ; he thought it was a whimsical fancy, and he did not doubt but that he should soon bring her round by flattering words and beautiful presents. But when he found that she would not listen to his words, and that she refused his presents, he began to look more seriously on the matter, and complained to the emperor. Domitian was very angry when he learned that she was a Christian, and he ordered her to be brought before his tribunal. Then this gentle and timid girl, who had never before appeared in public, and had always been treated with the greatest respect and kindness, was roughly seized and brought a prisoner into a public court of justice. Domitian spoke to her in coarse, insulting language; he encouraged the people who were present to laugh at her and revile her, and he tried to frighten her by threatening to inflict the most horrible torments on her. But she remained quite unmoved; till at last Domitian, finding he could do nothing with her, gave her her choice, either to sacrifice immediately to the gods, or to be banished to the island of Pontia. The choice was made without a moment's hesitation, and Flavia Domitilla was sent off to Pontia.

In these days, when people have broken the laws, they were sometimes banished; and though it is a great punishment to them to be taken away from their homes and their families, and to be obliged to work very hard, yet they have the comfort of knowing that they will at all events meet with just and fair treatment. But it was quite different with those who were banished by the Roman emperors. They were put in charge of some wicked man, who thought only how he could make them most wretched; and he would often torture them, or kill them secretly if he knew that the emperor wished to get rid of them. This was the sort of way in which Flavia Domitilla was now treated. She was not allowed to see any of her friends; she was lodged in close, unhealthy rooms; she was fed with coarse, unwholesome food; she could not walk in the garden or move a step without being watched; she was treated

rudely by the servants and soldiers who waited on
her and guarded her; and if it was noticed that she
took pleasure in one thing more than another, she
was immediately deprived of it. Most people would
have been very much fretted by this sort of petty
persecution, carried on every day and all day long.
But Domitilla did not seem to notice or to feel the
things that were done to vex and annoy her. She
gave herself entirely into the hands of her dearest
Spouse, Jesus Christ, and she knew that whatever
happened to her was ordered by Him. When we
love a person very much we like to do what he
wishes; and so Domitilla was very happy to live in
close rooms, and to eat coarse food, and to be watched
by the soldiers, and treated rudely by the servants,
because she loved Jesus, and knew that it was His
will that these things should happen to her. She
had still one great consolation, which was the company of Nereus and Achilleus, who had followed her
to Pontia. They waited on her most affectionately;
they did all they could to make her more comfort-
able; and above all, they talked to her about Jesus,
who was so dear to them all.

After some time Aurelian came to see her, hoping to find that she was tired out with all that she
had suffered in her banishment, and was ready to
marry him. He was very much surprised to see
how calm and joyful she looked, and to hear her

talk of the great happiness she was enjoying, He looked round at the wretched room in which she was confined, and he was puzzled to think what could make her so happy where other people would have been very miserable. He saw, however, that she had still one consolation, which was the company of Nereus and Achilleus, and he was so selfish and cruel as to take them away from her.

As Nereus and Achilleus were only slaves, he might do whatever he liked to them. So he had them cruelly scourged, and then sent them to Terracina, to a friend of his, called Memmius Rufus, who was governor of the place, and he told him to punish them as severely as he could, because they were obstinate Christians. Memmius Rufus at first tried to persuade them to sacrifice to the gods; but they declared that nothing in the whole world would ever induce them to give up what the Apostle St. Peter had taught them. He, therefore, determined to see what would come of these words when they were put to the torture, and he ordered them to be placed on a horrible wooden machine, called the horse, which was used for torturing slaves. Here their limbs were drawn out of joint, and their sinews were strained to the farthest stretch, and at the same time plates of red hot iron were applied to their sides and other parts of their naked bodies, so as to burn them dreadfully. But in the midst of their agony they remained unmoved, and broke out into songs of triumphant joy as each fresh torture was inflicted on them. Memmius Rufus, at last, saw that it was hopeless to conquer their constancy and he had them beheaded.

Aurelian hoped that now that Nereus and Achilleus were gone, Domitilla would soon make up her mind to marry him, and to return to the gay life she used formerly to live at Rome. But he was again mistaken. Though Nereus and Achilleus had been a great comfort to Domitilla, yet it was in Jesus that her real strength and comfort lay; and now that He had been pleased to let her friends be taken from her, she looked only the more simply to Him for support and consolation. And so it came to pass that when Aurelian again visited her, expecting to find her dull and out of spirits, she was even more firm in her faith and more happy than she had been when he was there before.

Aurelian was now convinced that there was no hope of conquering Domitilla's obstinacy by keeping her in the island of Pontia, and so he determined to take her away and marry her by force. He, therefore, carried her with him to Terracina, and invited a large party to be present at his wedding. Aurelian and his friends began to feast and make merry, while poor Domitilla was shut up in a room alone, sad and trembling, waiting till Aurelian should come to her and force her to marry him. It seemed now that all hope was lost, and that she must at last be obliged to marry him. But still Domitilla's heart did not sink, and she continued to hope and trust in Jesus. She had vowed herself to Him, and she was sure that He would defend her, because she was His own spouse. She knelt and prayed in her solitary chamber, while the jovial party in the banqueting room drank and feasted. At last they began to dance, and Aurelian was the merriest of them all, dancing and laughing with all his might, and rejoicing to think that he had at last conquered this proud Christian girl. But in a moment the merry scene was changed. God struck Aurelian, and he fell down dead. Then there was a sudden cry of alarm, followed by a loud weeping and wailing, which ran through the house, and told Domitilla that our Lord had heard her prayer, and had delivered her from the great danger which had threatened her.

This was not, however, the end of all that Domitilla had to suffer for Jesus' sake. Luxorius, Aurelian's brother, was very angry with her, because he said that she had been the cause of his brother's death, and he accused her to Trajan, who at this time was emperor, and he got leave to question her, and put her to death if she would not sacrifice to the heathen gods He came to Terracina, where

8

she was living with two other young women, Theodora and Euphrosina, whom she had persuaded to
be Christians and to vow themselves to a life of
chastity.   They were all three brought before Luxorius, who told them that the emperor ordered
them to sacrifice to the gods, and he advised them
to obey at once, for if they did not, he would put
them to a cruel death.   They refused to do so, and
answered boldly and firmly to all he asked them
about their religion.   He knew there was little
chance of making Domitilla change her mind, and,
besides, he was not sorry to punish her for the
death of his brother.   So he ordered them all three
to be shut up in a room, which was then set on fire,
and thus they were burnt to death.   The next
morning Cesarius, a deacon, came to the place and,
on going to the room in which they had been shut
up, he found them dead, lying on the floor on their
faces, just as they had prostrated themselves in
prayer, but without a hair of their head being singed
or any part of their body being burned.   The fire
had released their souls from this mortal life, but it
had been miraculously prevented from burning
their bodies.   Cesarius took up their bodies and
buried them with great honor.   The church keeps
the feast of St. Flavia Domitilla, together with that
of SS. Nereus and Achilleus, on the 12th of May.

CHAPTER IX.

DEAR reader, I would wish from my soul that I could enkindle in your heart that divine fire which Jesus Christ came to cast on earth ; the fire of love—love of holy chastity. I would wish from my soul that I could implant in the heart of every one the snow-white lily of purity. This virtue is so pleasing to God, that the Holy Ghost cries out in a transport of joy: "O! how beautiful is a chaste soul in the light of glory." And, indeed, a chaste soul is purer than silver and brighter than the finest gold. She is a lovely and radiant star in the hand of the Most High. Bring together all that is beautiful in nature, and you will find that a chaste soul is more beautiful than all. How beautiful is the sweet light of morning, how beautiful are the varied tints of the rainbow, but a chaste soul is far more beautiful. The dazzling beams of the noonday sun are bright, indeed, but the light that beams from a pure soul is far brighter. The silvery stars glitter brightly in the dark blue sky, but a chaste soul glitters far more brightly. The spring-lily and the fresh fallen snow look white and pure, but the purity of a chaste soul is far whiter, for it is white with the purity of heaven.

There is a sublime and awful beauty in the rolling thunder, and in the vivid lightning, as it flashes through the dark clouds, but there is something far more sublime and awful in the beauty of a chaste soul. There is in her a majesty on which even angels gaze with fear and delight. So marvellously beautiful is a pure soul in the light of glory, that could we but gaze on her, we could die of joy; for such a soul is the living image of the living God. Pure, virgin souls are the fairest flowers in the garden of the church; they are the most cherished portion of the flock of Jesus Christ. The virtue of chastity is so noble that it elevates man above the laws of nature; it gives him a foretaste of heaven; it places him on a level with the angels. From an enemy of God, chastity makes man a friend of God; from a weak, sinful mortal, chastity makes him an angel.

Our divine Redeemer assures us that in heaven there shall be *no* marriage; the blessed in heaven shall not marry, or be given in marriage, but they shall be like the angels of God. Now, the chaste soul anticipates here on earth the life of heaven, and lives as an angel amid the dangers and corruption of this world. It is true there is a difference between an angel and a pure soul, but they differ in happiness *only* and not in virtue. The chastity of the angel is more happy, but the chastity of a pure soul is more heroic. Yes, I repeat it, if, though the chastity of the angels is happier, yet the chastity of a pure soul is more virtuous, more heroic. I know full well that the angels are most pure and sinless, but it is their nature to be so. The angels are pure spirits. They are free from all the restraints of matter; they are free from the miseries of this life; they live in heaven. They stand not in need of food, or drink, or sleep. They have not to wage continual war against wild, unruly passions—against the world, the flesh and the devil. The sweetest songs, the most ravishing melodies, cannot charm *them*. The fairest forms of earthly beauty cannot allure *them*. If, then, they are chaste, they are so without struggling, without suffering. But when weak man—sinful by nature, subject to a thousand wants, condemned to live in the midst of a corrupt world, with dangers within and dangers without, dangers on every side—when weak man struggles *bravely* against his very self, against the pleasures of the senses, against the charms of the world, against the allurements of the demons—when weak man struggles *untiringly* against his most deadly enemies,

8*

who cease not to tempt him, day or night, waking or sleeping, at work as in prayer, in the solitude of his chamber as on the busy street, and when, with the grace of God, man triumphs over all—triumphs through a long, weary life of ceaseless warfare—and lives as an angel, ah ! that is noble, that is heroic, that is *sublime*, that is *god-like*.

Yes, dear reader, a chaste soul is not only more bright and beautiful than all the beauties of nature, she is not only the brightest ornament of the holy church, she stands not only on a level with the angels; nay, she is superior to the angels—she is like unto God. No wonder, then, that the virtue of chastity is so much loved and admired by God and by men. Even the brute creation, even inanimate nature, loves and honors a chaste soul. We can find inumerable examples of this in the lives of the Saints. Whenever the blessed Agnes, of Monte Pulciano, went out walking in the garden or in the fields, the flowers began to bud and bloom around her, as if her very presence brought them the sunshine and the fresh air of Paradise. Whenever St. Francis of Assissi went to walk in the woods, the little birds fluttered around him and perched on his shoulders, and sang to him in their own tiny way the praises of God ; and then the Saint, full of joy, would caress them, call them his "dear little sisters," and then would give them his blessing. Even the wild beasts grew tame in the presence of this chaste soul. They forgot their fierceness, and obeyed his voice, as they obeyed, in days of old, the voice of Adam in the garden of Paradise. There is, dear reader, in the virtue of chastity something so beautiful, so majestic, so glorious, that even the heathens, even the fierce savages—nay, even the most corrupt and degraded hearts, dead to every sense of shame and honor, cannot help admiring and loving it. We can see from history how highly the virtue of chastity was honored by the corrupt pagan nations of Egypt and Rome, as well as by the savage tribes of ancient Gaul, and at the present day we hear, on every side, the cry of admiration which is wrung from the hearts of even the most bitter enemies of holy faith, by the pure lives of those ministering angels, the Sisters of Charity. See them during the late war, going through the hospitals, going through the midst of the dead and the dying, going unharmed through the midst of friends and foes. Where was the man so degraded, so brutalized, that dared insult the Sister of Charity? No! there was not one. Why was this universal respect? Ah! it was because they are virgins.

O, how beautiful is a chaste generation! Truly, it is esteemed, it is admired, it is loved by God and by man! The Holy Church, enlightened by the Holy Ghost, esteems so highly the virtue of chastity, that she requires it as an indispensable condition of all her servants. No one can ascend the steps of her altars and open the tabernacle in which Jesus reposes ; no one can bear the glorious Son of the Virgin Mary in triumphal procession ; none can call down the Eternal Son of God from the highest heavens ;—no one but the *priest*, and *he* must be a *virgin!* No one can preach the Word of God to encourage the good and to convert the sinner ; no one can strike off the chains of sin, in the tribunal of penance, and cleanse the soul in the precious blood of Jesus Christ; no one can administer that Heavenly Food which is the life to the world; no one can prepare the soul for its fearful passage into eternity—I repeat it, no one but the *priest,* and he must be *chaste* ; he must be a *virgin.* Do you not see, then, my dear reader, that the salvation of the entire world depends in a certain degree upon the preservation of holy chastity ?

But not only does inanimate nature ; not only do the wild beasts ; not only do the most degraded men ; not only does the Holy Catholic Church honor and esteem the virtue of Chastity, God Himself honors and loves this virtue with a most special love. God is a most pure spirit, and the source of all purity. The Son of God is begotten eternally of the Father, and the Holy Ghost proceeds eternally from Father and Son, but this generation, this procession, is shrouded in the dazzling splendor of ineffable purity. When God created the world He placed His own seal upon His creatures, and this seal was—holy purity. The angels were the first works of His hands, and He made them pure and spotless. When God created our first parents and placed them in the garden of Eden, He created them pure and sinless virgins. And when the ever-blessed Son of God came upon the earth to ransom us, He chose for His *forerunner* a pure virgin, a virgin sanctified from His mother's womb, a virgin to whom the prophet had given the glorious title of "angel of God;" it was the great St. John the Baptist.

And of whom was Jesus born ? whom did Jesus choose before all others to be His mother ? Ah ! dear reader, you know it well; it was the Blessed among women—it was the stainless Lily, the ornament and glory of our race,—it was the Immaculate Virgin Mary. So greatly does God love and prize the virtue of holy chastity, that in order to preserve it unsullied in His blessed Mother, He superseded the laws of nature; He wrought an unheard of miracle, and Mary became a fruitful Mother and remained a spotless Virgin. And whom did Jesus choose before all men to be His foster father? Whom did He choose to be spouse and guardian of His Blessed Mother ? It was the humble St. Jo-

seph. St. Joseph was a virgin. Which of all the
disciples did Jesus love most tenderly ? Who was
it that rested his head upon the bosom of Jesus at
the last supper, and heard the throbbings of His
sacred heart? To whom did Jesus bequeathe His
own dear mother, as He hung expiring upon the
cross ? Ah! dear reader, it was no other than the
Evangelist of love—the virgin St. John. And who
were the first flowers—the first sweet roses of the
redemption ? They were the Holy Innocents and
the Virgin Martyr St. Stephen.   Even those among
the apostles who were married left their wives as
soon as Jesus called them to His service, and lived
ever after in holy chastity.

You know how great was the love which Jesus
bore to little children. He loved to see them around
Him ; and when the apostles wished to drive them
away, Jesus said : "Let those little children come
to Me."   Then Jesus would take the little ones in
His arms ; He would embrace them and bless them,
then He would say to those around Him : "Unless
you become as little children you cannot enter the
kingdom of heaven."   Jesus Christ assures us that
the guardian angels of little children are always
gazing in the face of His Heavenly Father, *i. e.*,
they are always praying for God's most special protection over those little ones.   Then Jesus pro-
nounces a most terrible woe against all those that

lead children into sin: "Woe to him," He says, "that scandalizes one of those little ones. It were better for him that a mill-stone were tied around his neck, and that he were drowned in the depths of the sea." Now, why does Jesus love children with such a special love? Why does He watch over them with such tender care! Why does He guard and protect them with more than mother's love? Ah, dear reader, it is because children are yet pure, because they are yet innocent.

But even if we had no other proof of the unspeakable beauty, the inestimable value of holy chastity, the example of our Divine Saviour *alone* would draw all hearts irresistibly to love this angelic virtue. Jesus Himself, as you know, was a virgin, and He loved His virginity with a jealous love. Our Blessed Redeemer was the most meek and humble of men. The perfidious Jews sought to blacken His character by the foulest calumnies, and He bore it *all* with patience. They called Him a heretic and a false prophet. They sneered at Him on account of His poverty; they called Him a Galilean, a carpenter, and the son of a carpenter. They treated Him as an ignorant clown, as a madman, and even as one possessed by the devil. Those wicked men were not ashamed to tell our dear Lord to His face that He was a sorcerer and a minister of Satan. Our Blessed Redeemer bore all these sneers and calumnies with the patience of a God. But there was one sin—one stain that He never suffered to be branded upon His character, and that was the stain of *impurity.* *Never* did His most bitter enemies dare to accuse Him of such a sin. Nay, He challenged them publicly; He defied them to their teeth to convict Him of any sin, or even the least shadow of a sin, against this holy virtue, *so* dear to His heart was this heavenly virtue, so jealous was He of the honor of holy Purity.

O holy, O lovely, O divine virtue of Purity, how wonderful, how amiable, how beautiful must thou be, since thou hast captivated the heart of God Himself! Yes, dear reader, the beauty of holy Chastity has so enamoured the heart of Jesus that He has chosen the most endearing words that language can find to express His ardent love for pure souls. When Jesus speaks to *ordinary* Christians, He calls them His servants and He is their Master. When He speaks to faithful and obedient souls, He calls them His sheep and He is their Shepherd. When He speaks to His beloved disciples, He calls them His friends, His brethren; but, when He speaks to the chaste soul—ah! then He uses far more tender language—He calls her His sister, His spouse, ''Soror mea, Sponsa.'' He calls her His ''sister,'' for His love is pure as a sister's love. He calls her His *spouse,* for His love is always tender and ardent as the love of a bridegroom for His bride.

Long ago God uttered a remarkable prophecy: "I shall espouse thee forever, said the Lord; I shall espouse thee in justice; I shall espouse thee in mercy; I shall espouse thee in faith." This prophecy was not *then* understood; but when the Son of God came upon earth to establish a new race of virgins, then it was that this prophecy was not only understood but fulfilled, and its fulfilment continues, and will continue to the end of time.

In order to show us the reality of these spiritual espousals, our Divine Redeemer has often appeared to chaste souls, in a visible form, and espoused them in a sensible manner. One day, during the time of carnival, the pious virgin, St. Catharine, of Sienna, was praying in her cell. Her relatives and neighbors were amusing themselves, according to the custom of the season; but she sought her pleasure in God alone. On a sudden our Blessed Saviour appeared to her and said: "Because thou hast shunned the vanities and forbidden pleasures of the world, and hast fixed thy heart on Me alone, I shall now espouse thee in faith and unite thy soul to Mine." Then St. Catharine looked up and saw beside our Saviour the Blessed Mother of God. She also saw there St. John, the Evangelist, St. Paul, the Apostle, and St. Dominic, the founder of

the order.   The prophet David, too, was present at
her espousal, and he played on his harp with mar-
vellous sweetness.   The Blessed Virgin Mary now
took the right hand of St. Catharine and presented
her to our Blessed Saviour.   She besought her
divine Son to accept this virgin for His spouse.
Then Jesus smiled graciously upon the Saint.   He
drew forth a golden ring, set with four precious
stones, in the centre of which blazed a magnificent
diamond.   He then placed this ring upon the finger
of St. Catharine and said: "I, thy Creator and
Redeemer, espouse thee in faith.   Be faithful until
death, and we shall celebrate our nuptials in heaven."
The vision disappeared, but the ring remained on
the finger of St. Catharine.   She could always see
it; but by a special grace it was invisible to others.

O chaste souls, I speak especially to you, whose
hearts are yet pure and unsullied — to you, whose
souls are yet gleaming with the glory of virginity.
O, for the love of Jesus, be mindful of your dignity.
Remember that in the holy sacrament of Baptism
you became the living temples of the living God,
and the Holy Ghost took up his dwelling in your
hearts.   You became children of God, heirs of
heaven, and spouses of Jesus Christ.   Yes! This
is the dignity to which God has called you.   And
who is Jesus — who is this heavenly Bridegroom,
Who wishes to claim your hearts? Ah! you know

it already ; He is the glorious Son of the Virgin Mary, conceived in her chaste womb by the power and operation of the Holy Ghost. He is beautiful —the most beautiful of the children of men. He is white and ruddy, chosen out of thousands. His is a beauty that never wearies, a beauty which age can never alter—that never fades. His beauty is the joy of the blessed in heaven ; it is a beauty on which the angels gaze with ever-flowing delight. All the beauty of earth and heaven is but a feeble ray of His unutterable beauty.

Jesus is loving. O, how faithful, how ardent, is the love of Jesus Christ ! He has loved you from all eternity. He has made every sacrifice to win your love. He has loved you unto death, to the death of the cross. He will never abandon you, unless you yourself cast Him from you ; and when, at the hour of death, the nearest and dearest forsake you, then will Jesus stand at your side ; He will console you and deliver your soul from the hands of your enemies.

And Jesus *is powerful.* He is King of kings and Lord of lords ; He is the Judge of the living and the dead. He is the Creator of all things, visible and invisible. He is God. At His name every knee must bend in heaven, on earth, and in hell. The heavens above are His throne ; the earth beneath His footstool. At His touch the sick are healed, and the dead restored to life. He speaks, and the wild winds grow calm; the foaming waves subside at His voice. He calls the stars by name, and they answer to His call. Thousands of angels minister unto Him, and a thousand times ten thousand angels surround Him, and await His bidding in trembling awe.

And Jesus is *rich*. All the gold of the mountains, all the pearls of the ocean, are His. His are all the treasures of earth, and sea, and sky. He opens His hand and all creatures are filled with His blessings.

The holy virgin martyr, St. Agnes, was sought in marriage by a rich and powerful youth of Rome. When she heard his proposal, she answered: "Begone from me, food of death! My heart already belongs to another." Then the young nobleman, who loved her passionately, offered her countless treasures. He offered her gold, and pearls, and precious stones, and costly garments. He offered her all the honors, all the wealth he had inherited from his ancestors. The virgin smiled in pity at such an offer. "You offer me riches," she answered, "and my bridegroom possesses all the treasures of earth and heaven. He has placed on my finger the bridal ring. He has given me the bridal robe more costly than the queens of earth can wear. He has adorned my ears with glittering jewels, and my neck with costly pearls. He has placed on my brow a bridal crown, whose glory shall never fade, and His blood is upon my cheek." When at length the holy virgin was condemned to die, because she would not renounce her heavenly bridegroom, Jesus, she went with joy to the place of death like a bride hastening to the marriage feast. All who saw her wept; but Agnes *did not* weep. The hands of the executioner trembled, his face grew pale, and the tears started unbidden to his eyes; but Agnes smiled, for she feared not death. "Why do you wait?" she cried; "strike, and let me die for Him who has died for me! Strike! and let this body perish, which can be loved by another than Him, whom I love." Then the virgin raised her eyes and hands to heaven and said: "O Jesus, I have yearned for Thee; now I behold Thee. I have hoped in Thee; now I possess Thee. I have loved Thee on earth; now I shall love Thee forever in heaven." Then the youthful virgin knelt and bowed her head. With her own tiny hands she turned aside her long golden hair, and bared her neck to the blow, and Agnes remained *a virgin* and received the martyr's crown.

O, dear reader, who is there that would not love such a bridegroom as Jesus? Well might even the angels envy the happiness that is granted to us frail and sinful mortals. The angels are but

9*

the ministers of Jesus ; chaste souls alone are His spouses. I know full well that all are not called to live in perpetual virginity ; but *all* are called to lead *pure lives;* all are called to observe chastity according to their state, for nothing impure can enter heaven. I know that all are not called to lead on earth the life of virgins, but I say *blessed* are they that are called. "Blessed are they that are called to the marriage feast of the Lamb." Blessed are they here on *earth*, blessed are they in *heaven !* All the joys and pleasures of this earth cannot be compared to the happiness of a pure soul.

A virgin is free from all the cares, the anxieties, the burdens of a married life. You, dear reader, know perhaps how bitter these cares and anxieties are, and that nothing but death can relieve them. Indeed, so great and so numerous are the miseries of married life, that could people have a year of noviceship before binding themselves to that state, I fear there would be but few vocations. If any one thinks that I exaggerate, I would refer him to the statistics, where he can find the number of divorces that have, within the past few years, been granted in our own enlightened Republic, as well as in the various parts of the civilized world.

Now, a virgin is free from all these cares. Her care, her only care, is to please her heavenly bridegroom, Jesus Christ, to make herself beautiful in

His eyes. She only thinks of *His* beauty, *His* mercy, *His* love. Jesus is her joy, her peace, her paradise. You would wish me, dear reader, to describe to you the pleasures of holy chastity, but I would ask you: Can you describe the sweetness of honey to one who has never tasted it? No! my dear reader, and neither can I describe to you the sweet pleasures of holy chastity, unless you yourself have tasted these pleasures. Language has no words to describe them to one who has never experienced them. But, believe me, the joys of holy chastity far surpass all the pleasures of the senses; all the joys of earth. If you wish, dear reader, to be convinced of what I say, then go, stand beside the death-bed of a pure soul; behold the calm joy that beams on her face, listen to the sweet song of gladness that flows from her lips.

When the Blessed Mary, of Oignies, was about to die, her soul was filled with such heavenly joy that she could no longer contain it within her breast. She burst forth into a melodious hymn of praise and gladness. For three days and three nights she continued to sing, and her voice only grew louder and stronger as she drew near her end; and it was sweet and clear as the voice of an angel. She continued thus to sing until her pure soul went forth to join in the melodious choirs of the blessed in heaven. Thus died this chaste soul, and thus, too, have thousands died who served God in holy chastity.

Now, I ask you : Can that soul have been sad and unhappy during life who can sing and rejoice at the hour of death ? Can he have feared pain or sorrow who smiles and exults in the very face of death ? Ah, my dear reader, to the chaste soul, death is a welcome messenger, who tells her that the Bridegroom calls, that the marriage feast is ready. And blessed, ah ! thrice blessed is he that is called to the marriage feast of the Lamb.

St. John was taken up in spirit to the summit of a lofty mountain, and there he beheld a faint glimpse of the unutterable glory that is reserved for virgins in heaven. "Behold," he says, "I saw a Lamb standing on Mount Sion and there were with him one hundred and forty-four thousand, who bore *His* name and the name of His Father, written on their foreheads. And I heard a sound from heaven. It was as the noise of many waters and as the sound of great thunder ; and the sound that I heard was as the voice of harpers playing on their harps. And they sang a new canticle before the throne ; and no one can sing that canticle but those who have been purchased from the earth. These are they who have never been defiled with women, for they are virgins, and they follow the Lamb withersoever he goeth."

O, dear reader, how great must be the glory of virgins in heaven! Star differs from star in brightness, but the radiant star of virginity shall shine with a brightness, that far exceeds all others. The virgins shall bear the name of the Lamb, the sweet name of Jesus, and the ineffable name of God, upon their forehead. They shall sing a canticle, which no one else can sing; a *new* canticle, a canticle far surpassing in sweetness and sublimity the melodies of the angels and the hymns of the rest of the blessed. And the virgins shall follow the Lamb whithersoever He goeth. Others, indeed, shall follow the Lamb, but the *virgins* shall be the nearest to their divine Bridegroom. All the blessed shall be filled with joy, and no one shall annoy the other; but of all the blessed, the virgins shall be the most intimately united to Jesus; they shall receive from Him as their Bridegroom the most tender marks of His love; they shall be the darlings of His sacred Heart, the foundlings of His Immaculate Mother.

O, dear reader, can there be one that does not love the heavenly virtue of holy chastity, a virtue which is so pleasing to God? I am sure that could you but understand the wondrous beauty of this god-like virtue, you would willingly sacrifice wealth, health and honors, nay, life itself, rather than lose the glorious crown reserved for virgins in heaven. But we carry this precious treasure in frail vessels, and we live amid the dangers of a corrupt world, with dangers within us, dangers without us; dangers from enemies, visible and invisible.

If, then, this virtue, if your immortal soul is dear to you, O for the love of Jesus, engrave these two words deeply in your heart: Watch and pray! Watch over your soul that no sinful thought may enter there, and should it enter unawares, cast it out instantly, as you would do a disgusting insect, or a spark of fire. Watch over your heart that no sinful affection may possess it. Watch over your eyes that they may not gaze on any pictures or books, or other objects, that could soil the lustre of your purity. Watch over your ears that they may listen to no immodest words, or words of double meaning. Watch over your tongue, and remember that your tongue has been sanctified in holy communion, by touching the virginal flesh and blood of Jesus Christ. Watch over your whole body, for your body is a temple of the Holy Ghost, consecrated in baptism, and he that pollutes a consecrated temple is accursed of God and His holy angels. Be watchful day and night, and avoid the occasion of sin. Avoid those persons and those places which are to you an occasion of sin. Flee from them as you would from a serpent; for he that loves danger shall perish in it. "If your eye be to you an occasion of sin, pluck it out and cast it from you, for it is better to go blind into the kingdom of heaven, than with both eyes to be cast into the pit of hell. And if your hands or your feet be to you an occasion of sin, cut them off and cast them from you, for it is better to go lame and maimed into the kingdom of God, than to have two hands and two feet to be cast into hell fire." These are the words of Jesus Christ, my dear reader ; He certainly knew what He was saying. You must *watch and pray.* You must pray to Jesus. Jesus is a jealous God and He commands you to call upon Him in the hour of temptation. You must hasten to the altar, and receive often into your heart the virginal flesh and blood of Jesus Christ. You must partake of the "wheat of the elect, and of the wine that maketh virgins ; for unless you eat of the flesh of the Son of Man and drink His blood, you shall have no life in you !" You must pray to *Mary,* the Queen of Virgins, the lovely standard-bearer of virginity. The very name of Mary is a sweet balm which heals and fortifies the soul. The very thought of Mary's immaculate purity is a check upon the passions. The love of Mary is a fragrant rose which puts to flight the foul spirit of uncleanness.

A young man who was very much addicted to the sin of impurity came once to confession to a certain priest. The good priest was very greatly afflicted on learning that the young man had always fallen again into this sin after every confession. He advised the young man to place himself entirely under the protection of the Blessed Virgin Mary. He told him to say a Hail Mary every morning and evening in honor of her immaculate purity, to kiss the ground three times, and to say: "O Mary, my Mother, I give myself entirely to thee this day; I consecrate to thee my eyes, my ears, my tongue, my heart and my whole body and soul. O protect me, for I am thine." And whenever he was tempted he should say: "O Mary, help me, for I am thine!" The young man followed this advice, and in a short time, he was entirely delivered from this accursed sin. Now, this same priest related this fact one day from the pulpit. Amid the audience there was an officer, who kept up a criminal intercourse with a certain person. As soon as he heard this fact, he also made the resolution to practice this devotion, in order to free himself from the shameful slavery in which he was bound. In a short time he, too, was entirely freed from the degrading vice of uncleanness. Some months after, however, he had the impudence to go again to the house of his companion in sin, as he wished to see whether she too had changed her life; but no sooner did he come before the door of the house, than a strange feeling of terror seized upon him, and he cried out: "O Mary, help me, I am thine!" That very instant he felt himself thrust back by an invisible hand and found himself at a distance from the house. He immediately recognized the danger in which he had been, and returned his most heartfelt thanks to God and to His holy Mother for having preserved him. Remember, then, to *watch and to pray.* Repeat again and again with the Holy Church: "Inflame, O Lord, our vains and hearts with the fire of Thy Holy Spirit, that we may serve Thee with a chaste body, and please Thee with a clean heart."

CHAPTER X.

IT is an article of our holy faith that the Son of God descended from heaven, became man and died on the infamous gibbet of the Cross for no other purpose than to save mankind from perpetual destruction. His whole life was devoted to this purpose. For this purpose alone he established His Church and called religious to be His co-operators.

Kings and monarchs of this world are bound to take good care of the temporal welfare of their subjects; but it belongs to religious, and it is their paramount duty, to work for the salvation and sanctification of their fellow-men. This it that gain which religious are allowed to make, nay, which must be the only object of all their thoughts, schemes, labors, sufferings and prayers.

As their divine vocation obliges them continually to work with all possible efforts for this great object, it is necessary for them to be enkindled with true zeal for the salvation of souls.

Now, what is the meaning of zeal for the salvation of souls? It is a desire to see God truly loved, and honored, and 'served by all men, so much so that those who are inflamed with this beautiful fire endeavor to communicate it to the whole world. If they perceive that God is offended, without their being able to put a stop to such offences, they weep and lament; they feel interiorly devoured and consumed by the fervor of their zeal. "Who should be looked upon as a man consumed with the zeal for the house of God?" asked St. Augustine. "He who ardently desires to prevent offences against God, and endeavors to repair such offences as he could not foresee, and who, when he cannot induce those who have sinned to weep, weeps and groans himself when he sees God dishonored." With such a zeal the saints of the Old Law were inflamed. "I found my heart and my bones," says Jeremiah (xx., 9, 10), "secretly inflamed, as with a fire that even devoured me ; and I fainted away, not being able to resist it; because I heard the blasphemies of many people." "I was inflamed with zeal for the God of armies," says Elias, "because the children of Israel have broken their covenant." (III. Kings xix., 10.) "A fainting has taken hold of me," says the royal Prophet, "because sinners have forsaken Thy law; and my zeal hath made me pine away, because my enemies forgot Thy commandments." (Psalms cxviii., 53.) These holy men were thus afflicted at seeing with what licentiousness the wicked violated the law of God; the sorrow of their minds passed into the humors of their body, and even into their very blood, as it were. "I beheld the wicked," says David, "I pined away; because they kept not Thy commandments." (Ps. 118, 158.)

"Mine eyes became fountains of water; because they observed not Thy law." *Ibid.* 136. It was the violence of his zeal that made David melt into tears when he beheld the infinite Majesty of God offended. This zeal made St. Paul write to the Romans: "I speak the truth in Christ, I lie not, my conscience bearing me witness in the Holy Ghost, that I have great sadness and continual sorrow in my heart; for I wished myself to be an anathema from Christ, for my brethren, who are my kinsmen according to the flesh." (Rom. ix. 1–3.)

How much have the saints not done for the salvation of their neighbors? Let us hear what the great Apostle of the Gentiles says of his own labors, troubles and sufferings for the salvation of men. In his epistles to the Corinthians he writes as follows: "Even unto this hour we both hunger and thirst; and are naked, and are buffeted, and have no fixed abode; and we labor with our own hands: we are reviled and we bless; we are persecuted and we suffer it; we are blasphemed and we entreat: we are made as the refuse of this world, the offscouring of all even until now." (I. Cor. iv., 11, 13.) "Our flesh had no rest, but we suffered all tribulation: combats without, fears within." (ii. Cor. vii., 5.) "In many more labors, in prisons more frequently, in stripes above measure, in deaths often. Of the Jews five times did I receive forty stripes, save one. Thrice was I beaten with rods; once I was stoned; thrice I suffered shipwreck; a night and a day was I in the depth of the sea. In journeying often, in perils of water, in perils of robbers, in perils from my own nation, in perils from the Gentiles, in perils in the city, in perils in the wilderness, in perils in the sea, in perils from false brethern. In labor and painfulness, in much watchings, in hunger and thirst, in fastings often, in cold and nakedness." (II. Cor. xi., 23–27.)

All truly apostolic men can speak a similar language. Were a St. Francis Xavier to appear in our midst, he could tell us how, for the sake of the barbarians, he climbed mountains and exposed himself to innumerable dangers to find those wretched beings in the caverns, where they dwelt like wild beasts, and lead them to God.

A St. Francis de Sales would tell us how, to convert the heretics of the province of Chablais, he risked his life by crossing a river every day for a year, on his hands and knees, upon a frozen beam, that he might preach the truth to those stubborn men

A St. Fidelis would tell us how, to bring back to God the heretics of a certain place, he willingly consented, in preaching to them, to lose his life.

"Ah," exclaimed St. Mary Magdalen de Pazzi, "how great a pain it is, O Lord, to see how one could help Thy creatures by dying for them and not be able to do so." In her zeal for the salvation of souls, she went so far as to desire to endure even the pains of hell for their conversion, provided she could still love God in that place, and God granted her wish by inflicting on her most violent pains and infirmities for the salvation of sinners ; and yet after all this, she shed bitter tears, thinking she did nothing for their conversion "Ah, Lord, make me die," she used to exclaim, "and return to life again as many times as is necessary to satisfy Thy justice for them."

The Curé of Ars, in one of his catechetical instructions, relates as follows : "A great lady of one of the first families in France has been here, and she went away this morning. She is rich, very rich, and scarcely twenty-three. She has offered herself to God for the conversion of sinners and the expiation of sin. She mortifies herself in a thousand ways, wears a girdle all armed with iron points; her parents know nothing of it; she is as white as a sheet of paper."

"And there came in my heart, as a burning fire, shut up in my bones, and I was wearied, not being able to bear it," says Jeremiah xx., 9.

No doubt, says St. John Chrysostom, "one man alone, inflamed with zeal for God's honor, is sufficient to convert a whole nation." (Homil. i. ad propul.) Witness the Prophets Elias, Eliseus, Isaias, St. John the Baptist and other Prophets.

Witness St. Bernard, who was like a fire that takes hold of a forest and destroys it completely. Such were the effects of his preaching that mothers prevented their children, wives their husbands, and friends their friends from going to listen to him, because the Holy Ghost gave such force to his words as would destroy all irregu'ar desires and affections in the hearts of his hearers.

Witness St. Dominic, who, like an angel from heaven, urged all on, by his words, life and example, to seek the kingdom of God; being enkindled with the fire of divine love he tried to enkindle the same fire in the hearts of all men. Upon being asked from what book he took such fiery sermons: "From the book of charity," he replied.   "This is the only book I study, and from it I take, not inflating, but inflaming words."

Witness St. Francis, of Assisium, of whom St. Bonaventura relates, that men of every age and sex ran to see and hear this man of God; for his words were like a burning fire penetrating to the innermost of the heart, and filling with admiration the minds of all his hearers.   His heart, his soul, his looks, his words, his actions, were all fire.   Hence the conversion of so many thousands from a sinful to a Christian life, and from a Christian life to a life of great perfection.

To please Jesus Christ it is neccessary for religious to be inflamed with similar zeal for the salvation of souls.

There is nothing more pleasing to God, or even so pleasing, as zeal for His glory and for the salvation of souls.   "We cannot offer any sacrifice to God," says St Gregory, "which is equal to that of the zeal of souls."   "There is no service," says St. John Chrysostom, "more agreeable to Him than this.   To employ one's life in this blessed labor is more pleasing to the Divine Majesty than to suffer martyrdom."   "And there is nothing," says Richardus, "that pleases God so much as the zeal of gaining souls."   This made St. Teresa say, "that she felt greater envy for those who were engaged in the salvation of souls, than for the martyrs. The reason of this is, because there is nothing so pleasing to God as charity;" for as St. Paul says, "charity is the greatest of virtues, and the bond of perfection." (I. Cor. xiii., 13.) Now, the zeal of which we speak is nothing else than ardent charity, which makes us not only love God with all our heart and serve Him with all our strength, but makes us also wish that the whole world might love and serve God in the same manner, and that His name might be glorified by all men, and that His kingdom might be established everywhere. To feel exceedingly great joy at whatever contributes towards God's glory, and to be penetrated with sorrow at all the sins which are committed, is an unspeakably great love of God. Indeed, a good son takes nothing more to heart than the honor and advancement of his father; his only joy and comfort is, to see his father advanced; all offences and outrages committed against him, are felt by him as keenly, nay, sometimes even more keenly, than if they were committed against himself. So, in like manner, all those who are inflamed with true zeal for the glory of God place and seek all their joy in seeing God honored and praised by the whole world; and nothing gives them more pain than to witness contempt for the Majesty of God.

It cannot be doubted that this zeal is a most

perfect act of the love of God. It is likewise a most excellent act of the love of our neighbor; for, as the love of God consists in rejoicing at whatever conduces to His glory, and in being afflicted at whatever offends Him; so, in like manner, true love for our neighbor consists in rejoicing at his welfare, and in sympathizing with him in his misfortunes, and in trying to prevent or remedy them to the best of our power.

Now, what can be a greater evil or misfortune for our neighbor than sin? The Saints say that, if we wish to know whether we love our neighbor, we should examine ourselves as to whether we are afflicted for his faults, and filled with joy at his spiritual advancement. "Who is weak," says the Apostle, "and I am not weak? Who is scandalized, and I am not on fire?" Who is he, says the Gloss on this passage, that becomes weak in faith, or in any other virtue, without my being afflicted for him, as I would be for myself; and who is in adversity, who is scandalized, or in trouble, and I feel not myself burnt up with tenderness and compassion? (II. Cor. xi., 29) St John Chrysostom says, "that the zeal for the salvation of souls is of so great a merit before God, that to give up all our goods to the poor, or to spend our whole life in the exercise of all sorts of austerities, cannot equal the merit of this zeal. The spiritual works of mercy surpass in value the corporal works of mercy as much as the price and value of the soul exceeds that of the body." "Would. you not feel hapyy," says this Saint," if you could spend large sums of money in corporal works of mercy ? But know, that he who labors for the salvation of . souls does far more ; nay, the zeal of souls is of far greater merit before God than the working of miracles. What great miracles did not Moses perform when the children of Israel went out of Egypt ? yet all that is nothing if compared to that ardent zeal which he testified, when, interceding for them with God, he said : "Either pardon them this trespass, or if Thou do not, strike me out of the book that Thou hast written". (Exod. xxxii, 31 – 32.) "Behold here," continues St. John Chrysostom, "the greatest miracle that Moses ever wrought."

Shall I say more to excite in us this holy zeal for the glory of God and the salvation of souls ? "The charity of .Christ urgeth us." (II. Cor. v., 14.) What! I hear the Son of God exclaim : "God so loved the world as to give His only begotten Son." (John III., 16.) I see Jesus Christ weep on straw ; I see Him weep over Jerusalem ; I see Him sweat blood ; I see Him scourged, crowned with thorns, carrying His cross ; I see Him lifted up on the cross between heaven and earth, between two malefactors ; I see Him suffer for mankind so much that even the sun cannot bear it — that even the rocks burst asunder; and my heart shall not feel moved at this spectacle of divine love and zeal of Jesus Christ. I hear Jesus Christ exclaim: "Father, forgive them;" "I thirst," *i. e.*, I thirst for the salvation of souls, and this cry of Jesus Christ from the cross shall not pierce my heart, and enkindle it with similar thirst for the salvation of souls?

What! I see a soul, nay, thousands of souls, ready to perish; I see them ready to fall into hell; I think that God died so ignominious and so painful a death for them; I see that it is in my power to do so much for their salvation, and I should remain idle, and I should not exert myself to the best of my power to save them even at the loss of my life! O, what great cruelty, my brethren! We hear a little child weeping, and we at once try to console it; we hear a little dog whining at the door, and we open it. A poor beggar asks for a piece of bread, and we give it. And we hear Jesus Christ *weeping* and crying for souls, and His voice makes no impression; we say with the man in the Gospel: "Trouble me not, the door (of our heart) is now shut. I cannot rise and give thee." (Luke xi.) If an ass, says our Lord, falls into a pit, you will pull him out even on a Sabbath day; and a soul, nay, thousands of souls, fall into hell every day, and shall we be like that ungodly Bishop of Burgos, who, on being told by Las Casas that seven thousand children had perished in three months, said: "Look you, what a droll fool; what is this to me and what is it to the king?" To which Las Casas replied: "Is it nothing to your lordship that all these souls should perish? Oh, great and eternal God! And to whom then is it of any concern?" (Life of Las Casas, by Arthur Helps.) Is our heart hard enough to listen with indifference to these words of the Gospel: "Begone, ye cursed, into fire everlasting."

.Must we not say to ourselves what St. Alphonsus was wont to say to himself to stir up his zeal for the salvation of souls: "Who knows," said he, "what God requires of me? Perhaps the predestination of certain souls may be attached to some of my prayers, penances, and good works." (Life, i. vol., p. 259.) What shall we answer if accused before the tribunal of God by those souls who have been lost by our want of zeal for their salvation? If one shall say: my soul would be saved had you prayed more on such and such an occasion? If another will say: my soul would enjoy God forever, had you come sooner to avert by works of penance the wrath of God; or if another says: a hunter spends whole days in cold and snow to hunt up some game, and perhaps finds it not, and you would have easily found and gained my poor soul for

9

heaven had you taken but a little more trouble for it, which you could have done so easily, instead of spending your time in vain and frivolous, nay, even sinful conversations! Alas! what answer shall we have to give? "And he was silent." (Math. xxii.)

To be destitute of this ardent zeal for the salvation of souls is to see, with indifferent eyes, the blood of Jesus Christ trodden under foot; it is to see the image and likeness of God lie in the mire, and not care for it; it is to despise the Blessed Trinity: the Father Who created it—the Son Who redeemed it—the Holy Ghost Who sanctified it; it is to belong to that class of shepherds, of whom the Lord commanded Ezekiel to prophesy as follows: "Son of man, prophesy concerning the shepherds of Israel; prophesy and say to the shepherds: Thus saith the Lord God: Woe to the shepherds of Israel — My flock you did not feed; the weak you have not strengthened; and that which was sick you have not healed; that which was broken you have not bound up, and that which was driven away you have not brought again; neither have you sought that which was lost; and My sheep were scattered, because there was no shepherd, and they became the prey of all the beasts of the field; and were scattered. My sheep have wandered in every mountain and in every high hill; and there was none, I say, that sought them. Therefore, ye shepherds, hear the word of the Lord : Behold, I myself come upon the shepherds, I will require my flock at their hand." (Ezek. xxxiv., 2, 11.) To be destitute of this zeal, is to hide the five talents which the Lord has given us, instead of gaining other five talents. Surely the Lord will say : "And the unprofitable servant cast ye out in the exterior darkness. There shall be weeping and gnashing of teeth." (Math. xxv., 30.)

What a shame for a religious to know that the devil, in alliance with the wicked, is at work, day and night, for the ruin and destruction of souls, and to be so little concerned about their eternal loss, just as if it was not true what the holy Fathers say, that the salvation of one soul is worth more than the whole visible world ! Since when is it, then, that the price of souls has been lessened ? Ah, as long as the price of the blood of Jesus Christ remains of an infinite value, so long the price of souls will remain the same also. Heaven and earth will pass away, but this truth will not. The devil knows and understands it but too well. Oh ! how he delights in a religious who is called by Jesus Christ "the hireling, because he has no care for the sheep, and who seeth the wolf coming and leaveth the sheep and flieth." (John x., 12.)

On the day of judgment, such religious will be confounded by that poor man of whom we read in

the life of St. Francis de Sales, as follows : One
day this holy and zealous pastor, on a visit of his
diocese, had reached the top of one of those dreadful mountains, overwhelmed with fatigue and cold,
his hands and feet completely benumbed, in order
to visit a single parish in that dreary situation ;
while he was viewing, with astonishment, those
immense blocks of ice of an uncommon thickness,
the inhabitants who had approached to meet him,
related that some days before a shepherd, running
after a strayed sheep, had fallen into one of these
tremendous precipices.   They added that his fate
would never have been known if his companion, who
was in search of him, had not discovered his hat on
the edge of the precipice.   The poor man, therefore, imagined that the shepherd might be still re-
lieved ; or if he should have perished, that he
might be honored with a Christian burial.   With
this view he descended, by means of ropes, this
icy precipice, whence he was drawn up, pierced
through with cold, and holding in his arms his
companion, who was dead, and almost frozen into a
block of ice.   Francis, hearing this account, turned
to his attendants, who were disheartened with the
extreme fatigues which they had every day to encounter, and availing himself of this circumstance
to encourage them, he said : "Some persons imagine that we do too much; and we certainly do far

less than these poor people. You have heard in what manner one has lost his life, in an attempt to find a strayed animal; and how another has exposed himself to the danger of perishing in order to procure for his friend a burial, which, under these circumstances, might have been dispensed with. These examples speak to us in forcible language; by this charity we are confounded, we who perform much less for the salvation of souls entrusted to our care, than those poor people do for the security of animals confided to their charge." Then the holy Prelate heaved a deep sigh, saying: "My God, what a beautiful lesson for Bishops and Pastors! This poor shepherd has sacrificed his life to save a strayed sheep, and I, alas! have so little zeal for the salvation of souls! The least obstacle suffices to deter me and make me calculate every step and trouble. Great God! give me true zeal and the genuine spirit of a good shepherd! Ah! how many shepherds of souls will not this herdsman judge!" Alas! how just and how true is this remark! If we saw our very enemies surrounded by fire, we would think of means to rescue them from the danger; and now we see thousands of souls, redeemed at the price of the blood of Jesus Christ, on the point of being cast into the eternal flames of hell; and shall we be less concerned and less active for these images and likenesses of God than for their frames, *i. e.*, their bodies?

My dear reader, are we not under an infinity of obligations to God ? Has He not created us ? Has He not redeemed us by His Blood ? Has He not had the goodness not to punish us for our sins, waiting for the hour of our repentance ? Does He not daily heap upon us benefits great in quantity, infinite in quality, pure in intention, and continual in their duration ? In a word, do not all good and perfect gifts proceed from the Most High, the Father of Light ? What return shall we make for them ? Behold, my dear reader, He transfers to our brethren the right to all we owe Him. He fully discharges us of every claim, on condition that we do all in our power for the salvation of our neighbor ?

Besides, how great is not the number of our own sins?—how enormous is not their weight?—how heinous their nature ? How shall we cover and cancel them ? One of the best means to satisfy the justice of God for all our offences is, to make efforts that others may cease to offend Him, and serve Him with all their heart. It is the apostle St. James, who says so: "He who makes a sinner forsake the errors of his life, will save the soul of the sinner, and cover a multitude of his own sins."(James v.,20.) St. Augustine takes notice of this truth upon the occasion of the cure of the possessed person in the Gospel. The holy text says that this man, seeing himself cured, wished to follow Jesus Christ, in acknowledgment of the great benefit he had received; but our Saviour did not permit him, but said to Him: "Return home and recount the wonders that God has wrought in thee, and he went about the town preaching the wonders that Jesus had wrought in him." (Luke viii., 39.)

What God requires of you in acknowledgment of the favor He has conferred on you, by drawing you out of the abyss of your sins is, to endeavor to draw your neighbor also out of sin and to urge him to serve God with all his heart.

Let us not be surprised at this. We all know but too well that sin is the greatest of all evils. In like manner, the remission of sin is the greatest of all good. By sin, the infinite Majesty, Bounty and Sanctity of God are most grievously offended; sin is a certain deicide, as it were, nay, it really and truly was a "Christicidium," for it could not be expiated by any other price than that of the blood and death of Jesus Christ. Now, this remission of sin can be operated only by the infusion of the grace of God, by which we become the children and heirs of God, and even the partakers of the divine nature, according to what St. Peter tells us. (Epist. 2., c. i., 4.) For this reason the Prophet Micheas exclaims: "Quis Deus similis tui, qui aufers iniquitatem!" For the justification of the impious soul is a greater work of God than the creation of the whole world. "Majus opus est ex impio justum facere, quam creare cœlum et terram," says St. Augustine, a truth which St. Thomas proves by saying that the least degree of sanctifying grace is worth more than the whole visible world. "Bonum gratiae unius hommis majus est, quam bonum naturæ totius universi," (St. Thom. p. g. 113, art. 9.) because, says St. Bernard, (Medit) God would not have given His life for the whole visible world; He delivered Himself up to an ignominious death only for the soul of man.

Moreover, God does not only take away sin from the soul, and deliver it from the worst of enemies that can attack and possess it, but He removes sin from the soul so far that, according to the prophet Micheas (c. vii.) ; He casts it into the depth of the sea, nay, on the day of judgment He will cast it, together with all sinners, into the abyss of hell.

All penitent Saints have always exalted and praised God for this admirable grace and gift. St. Peter would melt into tears whenever he heard the cock crow, remembering his denial of Christ; this fault was for him a perpetual incentive to give himself up entirely to the preaching, love and service of Christ; even unto the death on the cross for Christ. Hence he exults and rejoices at this grace, and congratulates the Gentiles upon it when he writes in his I. epist., chapt. 2, 9 : "You are a chosen generation, a kingly priesthood, a holy nation, a purchased people, that you may declare His virtues; Who hath called you out of darkness into his marvelous light: Who, in time past, were not a people, but are now the people of God. Who had not obtained mercy: but now have obtained mercy."

St. Paul, too, was altogether enraptured about his conversion, and congratulated himself upon it so much that he could not help exclaiming: "A faithful saying and worthy of all acceptation, that Christ Jesus came into this world to save sinners, of whom I am the chief; but for this cause have I obtained mercy, that in me first Christ Jesus might show forth all patience, for the information of them that shall believe in Him unto life everlasting. Now, to the King of ages, immortal, invisible, the only God, be honor and glory forever and ever. Amen. (I Tim. i., 15–18.)

St. Magdalen having been assured by our Lord Jesus Christ that her sins were forgiven, retired into solitude, there to spend her whole life in shedding tears of sorrow and love, of thanksgivings, in making acts of love, in prayer and contemplation, saying, with the spouse in the canticles: "A bundle of myrrh is my beloved to me;—compass me about with apples, because I languish with love. (Capt. I, 12, II, 5.)

St. Mary, of Egypt, likewise spent forty-seven

years in solitude, always remembering the following passage of Holy Scripture : "The mercies of the Lord I will sing forever."

If we have imitated these Saints in offending God, let us also imitate them in pacifying Him, by serving Him in the spirit of penance, of humility, of thanksgivings, of love and fervor; but especially by trying, to the best of our power, to rescue souls from the abyss of sin, and offer them in compensation for the evil we have done. Certainly, if we truly repent of our sins, if we are truly grateful for their remission, we shall most assuredly rejoice with such Saints in sacrificing to God's honor and the salvation of souls, our lives and whatever we have received of His bounty. With our whole strength we shall consecrate all our faculties eternally to the glorious and holy functions of divine love. We shal pray and labor without intermission that God alone may reign in our own soul; that all tongues may never cease to sound forth His praises, and that all creatures may have but one heart; we shall ardently desire always to be employed with the angels and blessed spirits in doing His will, in loving Him, and in glorifying His adorable name. There will be no danger to which we shall not be ready to expose ourselves, in order that our soul may be converted. We shall be glad even to lay down our life a thousand times, were it possible, to hinder one offence against the divine Majesty. I repeat again, if it be to us a subject of perpetual tears and compunction, ever to have offended so good a God and so kind a Redeemer, then, no doubt, we shall make the first petition in the Our Father the object of our perpetual desires and tears, viz : that the God of our heart and of all creatures may be known, perfectly loved, and faithfully served by all; and we shall never cease earnestly to invite, with the royal prophet, all creatures with their whole strength, and with all their powers, to magnify the Lord with us; but above all it will be our principal care, and most earnest prayer, that we ourselves may perfectly attain to this happiness of devoting to God all the affections of our soul and all the actions of our life.